D1600743

AMBITION:
FRIEND OR ENEMY?

POTENTIALS
GUIDES FOR PRODUCTIVE LIVING

Wayne E. Oates, General Editor

AMBITION: FRIEND OR ENEMY?

by

FREDERICK C. VAN TATENHOVE

THE WESTMINSTER PRESS
Philadelphia

Book design by Alice Derr

First edition

Published by The Westminster Press®
Philadelphia, Pennsylvania

PRINTED IN THE UNITED STATES OF AMERICA
2 4 6 8 9 7 5 3 1

Library of Congress Cataloging in Publication Data

Van Tatenhove, Frederick C.
  Ambition—friend or enemy?

  (Potentials)
  Bibliography: p.
  1. Ambition. I. Title. II. Series.
BJ1533.A4V36 1984   155.2′32   84-5199
ISBN 0-664-24530-7 (pbk.)

To
Janet

Who shares and shapes
my ambitions
with love and understanding

Contents

Foreword

The eleven books in this series, Potentials: Guides for Productive Living, speak to your condition and mine in the life we have to live today. The books are designed to ferret out the potentials you have with which to rise above rampant social and psychological problems faced by large numbers of individuals and groups. The purpose of rising above the problems is portrayed as far more than merely your own survival, merely coping, and merely "succeeding" while others fail. These books with one voice encourage you to save your own life by living with commitment to Jesus Christ, and to be a creative servant of the common good as well as your own good.

In this sense, the books are handbooks of ministry with a new emphasis: coupling your own well-being with the well-being of your neighbor. You use the tools of comfort wherewith God comforts you to be a source of strength to those around you. A conscious effort has been made by each author to keep these two dimensions of the second great commandment of our Lord Jesus Christ in harmony with each other.

The two great commandments are summarized in Luke 10:25-28: "And behold, a lawyer stood up to put him to the test, saying, 'Teacher, what shall I do to inherit eternal life?'

He said to him, 'What is written in the law? How do you read?' And he answered, 'You shall love the Lord your God with all your heart, and with all your soul, and with all your strength, and with all your mind; and your neighbor as yourself.' And he said to him, 'You have answered right; do this, and you will live.' "

Underneath the two dimensions of neighbor and self there is also a persistent theme: The only way you can receive such harmony of thought and action is by the intentional re-centering of your life on the sovereignty of God and the rapid rejection of all idols that would enslave you. The theme, then, of this series of books is that these words of Jesus are the master guides both to the realization of your own potentials and to productive living in the nitty-gritty of your day's work.

The books in this series are unique, and each claims your attention separately in several ways.

First, these books address great social issues of our day, but they do so in terms of your own personal involvement in and responses to the problems. For example, the general problem of the public school system, the waste in American consumerism, the health hazards in a lack of rest and vocational burnout, the crippling effects of a defective mental outlook, and the incursion of Eastern mystical traditions into Western Christian activism are all larger-than-life issues. Yet each author translates the problem into the terms of day-to-day living and gives concrete guidelines as to what you can do about the problem.

Second, these books address the undercurrent of helplessness that overwhelming epidemic problems produce in you. The authors visualize you throwing up your hands and saying: "There is nothing *anyone* can do about it." Then they show you that this is not so, and that there are things *you* can do about it.

Third, the authors have all disciplined themselves to stay off their own soapboxes and to limit oratory about how awful the world is. They refuse to stop at gloomy diagnoses of incurable conditions. They go on to deal with your potentials for changing yourself and your world in very specific ways. They do not let you, the reader, off the hook with vague, global utterances and generalized sermons. They energize you with a sense of hope that is generated by basic information, clear decision-making, and new directions taken by you yourself.

Fourth, these books get their basic interpretations and recommendations from a careful plumbing of the depths of the power of faith in God through Jesus Christ. They are not books that leave you with the illusion that you can lift yourself and your world by pulling hard at your own bootstraps. They energize and inspire you through the hope and strength that God in Christ is making available to you through the wisdom of the Bible and the presence of the living Christ in your life. Not even this, though, is presented in a namby-pamby or trite way. You will be surprised with joy at the freshness of the applications of biblical truths which you have looked at so often that you no longer notice their meaning. You will do many "double takes" with reference to your Bible as you read these books. You will find that the Bread of Life is not too holy or too good for human nature's daily food.

This volume, *Ambition: Friend or Enemy?,* is by Fred Van Tatenhove, Associate Professor of Pastoral Care and Counseling Coordinator, Department of Pastoral Ministry/Counseling Services, Asbury Theological Seminary. He is a new author with much to say to you on a topic we all think a great deal about within ourselves. Few of us speak aloud to each other about ambition; Joseph Epstein calls it a "secret passion." Fred Van Tatenhove breaks the secret out into the open in the only Christian book I know of on the subject. He sees ambition as native to all of us, neither friend nor enemy in and of itself. The kind of Christian commitment we have and the direction of that commitment determines whether ambition is an enemy or a friend, a means of self-destruction or a means of God's grace working through us as God's servants.

This book is steeped in the wisdom of contemporary psychology and sociology on the forms ambition takes in American life. For example, the author examines the way in which parents seek to live out their private ambitions in their children. He describes the "reverse ambition" of those whose fondest hope seems to be *not* to get anywhere in this world. These and many more psychological insights are set in the framework of a wise and perceptive interpretation of biblical truth. As you read this book you will think new thoughts, and I believe your life will find new directions for productive living as with godly ambition you express your potential.

WAYNE E. OATES

Louisville, Kentucky

Part I

TALKING OPENLY ABOUT A SECRET PASSION

Chapter 1

Let's Take a Look
at Our Ambitions

Art thou he that should come, or do we look for
another?

Matthew 11:3

Have you ever felt the dilemma of an honest question?
"Why did I get laid off? We were just getting on our feet financially." A question you want answered, but no answer
comes. "Where did I go wrong? I tried so hard to be a good
parent." You struggle with it. You tumble it over in your
mind late into the night. It won't go away. "How can there
be anything good in this; it is so painful?" You try to put it
to rest, but the next day there it is again. You take your
struggle to others, hoping to hear some answer that will relieve your tension. Honest questions, questions that leave
you in a dilemma. They are all too common for most of us.

The tough choices of one of these honest questions nagged
John the Baptist. "Art thou he that should come, or do we
look for another?" (Matt. 11:3). John was the New Testament prophet described as a "voice . . . crying in the wilderness." A lonely image indeed! His voice announced the public ministry of Jesus. John had more than a casual interest in
this man from Galilee. For one thing, they were second cousins. More than that, John felt the clear conviction to proclaim to his listeners that someone was coming "mightier
than I, whose shoes I am not worthy to bear" (Matt. 3:11).
John believed Jesus was that promised one. So strong was

this conviction that when word reached John describing the increasing popularity of Jesus over himself, he told his troubled followers that Jesus' popularity must increase and his own must decrease.

John's career was not without its dilemmas. As some would say, "He pulled no punches." His voice condemned King Herod's adulterous relationship with his brother's wife. This candid pronouncement got him into trouble. He was arrested, held in prison, and eventually put to death. In the isolation of his cell he began to question whether or not his ambition had gone for naught. He wondered if the desire that burned in his heart to see the "promised Son of Israel" had indeed been fulfilled. Honest questions began to form. Was Jesus the promised one? Was this son of a carpenter, born to Mary his mother's cousin, a friend or an enemy? The dilemma he felt can be heard in the question he sent with his followers to ask Jesus: "Art thou he that should come, or do we look for another?" From the day at the Jordan River, when John baptized Jesus, to John's imprisonment this question had become John's dilemma.

"What has all this to do with ambition?" you are asking. "I picked this book up because I am curious about ambition. I want to know, is it a friend or an enemy?"

These are honest questions, and when you relate them to ambition you are left with conflicts. How should I judge ambition—is it good, bad, or indifferent? Is it selfish to be ambitious? How should I look upon ambitious achievers? Are they to be admired or suspected? How can I control my ambitions? How do they differ from "win at all costs"? Do I need ambition to be successful? How does it fit the biblical teaching of servanthood? What is a Christian response to ambition? Should I flee from it as Shakespeare advised in *Henry VIII,* "Cromwell, I charge thee, fling away ambition, by that sin fell the angels"?

Where Does Ambition Come From?

Not much is known about the origin of ambition. Where does it come from? Is it caught, taught, or a natural part of one's personality? Why do some people burn with it, while others never seem to feel its heat? Even commonsense answers leave us in a dilemma. "Ambition comes from parents," you say. But where do parents get it? Is it passed on from generation to generation? Then why does one child get it and not the other brothers or sisters? I know parents who feel a lot of pain because a son or a daughter didn't "inherit" the ambition that they experience.

Others say, "It's the situation. One's background makes the difference." Is a child likely to be more ambitious if born to successful parents or to parents whose failures seem obvious? But what is success, what is failure? Are children born into homes of wealth more ambitious than those who grow up in some form of poverty? What do you think? For me, as I remember my boyhood days with patched overalls, darned socks, and hand-me-down clothes, I have no desire to duplicate that for my children. Those memories still make my ambition glow hotter.

"It's formed in the crucible of hardship," suggests another. That may be so. Orvis F. Collins thinks so. He noted in the book *The Enterprising Man,* a study of the founders of 110 companies, that an unusually large number of these men had lost a parent early in their lives. Is it possible that the "school of hard knocks" enhances one's ambitions? For some of you that was the key that unlocked your ambitious energies. Yet I believe, after hours of listening to the stories of those who carry emotional scars from losing parents by death or divorce early in their childhood, that the price is too high for the benefits gained. In my journeys with those who have experienced this kind of loss, I have yet to find anyone wishing these past experiences upon their children.

Have you noticed another curious dilemma? Ambition is unequally parceled out. It's a great divider of human beings. You can compare it to the biblical image of separating the sheep from the goats. There are those who have it and those who don't. Some, like sociologist Emile Durkheim, would argue that there is no in-between. Durkheim contends that ambitious types can't understand the less ambitious. They see the latter as losing their lives by not taking more responsibility for the "here and now." Those seen as less ambitious retort that it's the more ambitious who are sacrificing their inner selves to the outer world. Durkheim puts himself on the side of the ambitious ones. He believes that they experience a surer sense of direction, a firmer control over life, and a clearer stake in directing their future.

What Is Ambition Anyway?

In some circles ambition is not a word in "fine repute." It hasn't always been in vogue. In my search I found it was not even a central word in *Roget's Thesaurus* or in *Strong's Exhaustive Concordance of the Bible.* Actually, in the 1960s and 1970s ambition received a fairly poor press. Joseph Epstein, in his revealing book *Ambition: The Secret Passion,* observes, "To say of a young man or woman that he or she is ambitious is no longer, as it once was, a clear compliment. Rather the reverse."(*Ambition,* p. 3; see Selected Bibliography for the full reference for this and other quoted material.) There may be a slight ray of hope that ambition is becoming more respectable. The 1980s are experiencing an increased interest in self-starters. There's even an enterprising attitude developing, aided by the magazine *Venture: The Magazine for Entrepreneurs.* In an early issue, publisher Joseph D. Giarraputo described America as abounding in entrepreneurial activity, with some parts of the country attracting more than their share. One of these "entrepreneurial pockets" is clustered in

Santa Clara County in northern California. More than 1,500 high-technology firms headquartered there have earned that area the nickname of Silicon Valley. It's a hotbed of enterprising energy. Twenty of the fastest-growing companies of the top fifty started in the past ten years came from that small county.

The "spirit of Silicon Valley" will not warm the heart of everyone. There are some who equate ambition with aggression and therefore shiver in its presence. They view ambition as something you need to at least keep one eye on. Many watch the rearview mirror to be sure there are no flashing red lights following their ambition. They say, "Beware of ambition! Like the proverbial camel, once it gets its nose in the tent you must contend with the whole animal."

The truth is that many people mishandle ambition, others make ambition an end in itself, and some seem captured by a distorted need to achieve at any cost. But these expressions of ambition are more the result of distorted attitudes and values. The problem is not inherently in ambition but in the focus or purpose to which ambition is directed. Ambitious people are not by virtue of their ambition necessarily insensitive, selfish, and competitive. Some can be, but the difference is the purpose to which ambition is directed.

Ambition Defined

In its root meaning ambition is defined as an energy, expressed in active behaviors toward some purpose or aspiration. The aspiration or desire has an object. Ambition as an energy is focused on those objects. The historical meaning of the English word "ambition" comes from French and Latin roots. To the French root "amb," about, is added either the suffix "itus," going, or the suffix "ire," to go. Ambition is expressed in "going about." On the Latin side it began as a political term. The basic Latin form "ambitus" means going around a compass. The word originally described the practice of politicians going around to canvass citizens for votes.

Thus, an ambitious person was known as a go-getter. Harvey Sloane, mayor of Louisville, campaigned for the governor's office in 1980 in good Roman fashion by walking across the state of Kentucky so he could meet the people. Though this Roman strategy didn't help him win, going directly to the people has gained popularity among politicians in our impersonal society.

These early root meanings indicate that originally the word "ambition" was used to describe the actions of a person, not the motivations. A person desiring a political office was ambitious—a go-getter. Like many words it later became associated with moral values, but in its original usage ambition was not linked with worth or value, good or bad, right or wrong. It was merely a description.

By the fifteenth century, when the word "ambition" appeared in English literature, it meant "an eager desire for honour, rank, and position." Still later, Thomas Carlyle writes, "His ruin was that ambition had laid hold of him." Now the word was given negative value. The original emphasis upon the *act* of "canvassing," "going around," was replaced by the meaning "canvassing for *promotions*." A secondary definition became the meaning of primary usage. This switch is evident in the neutral work *Webster's Ninth New Collegiate Dictionary*, where the primary meaning describes ambition in a negative way with the original meaning listed afterward. However, the definitions for the words "ambition" and "ambitious" cited in the secondary positions are the most helpful: "the desire to achieve a particular end," "having a desire to achieve a particular goal." (By permission. From *Webster's Ninth New Collegiate Dictionary* © 1983 by Merriam-Webster, Inc., Publishers of the Merriam-Webster® Dictionaries.)

What is ambition, then? Epstein defines it as the "fuel of achievement." I like that image. Ambition is that part of your makeup which, when activated, provides you energy and motivation to achieve your goals and to fulfill your purposes.

Ambition Good, Bad, or Both

Picture ambition as a spark that requires fanning before it bursts into flame. Or see it as dormant energy which, when awakened, generates power that can change your destiny and direction. Like any energy, ambition can be used for either good or destruction. It can burn cleanly, without odor, or burn in a manner that gives off noxious fumes. Like a flame it can become a runaway fire or the focused heat of the glassblower's torch.

I once lived in a prime logging area in northern California. Each summer, fire patrols were flown daily to look for smoke. These patrols were not undertaken to keep fires from starting but to spot new fires before they got out of control. Occasionally, the thing we all feared would happen: a fire would become a "runaway." Even the established fire lines didn't always stop the unrestrained flames. Great sections of virgin timber that had required years of growth could be destroyed in a few hours. Ambition can be like that, a force that gets misdirected.

Have you watched glassblowers? They are only creative when they have a highly focused flame, finely adjusted with the right mixture of oxygen and acetylene. Ambition can be like that, a force that is channeled and focused. Ambition is part of your life, neither good nor bad, but a potential energy, poised for expression.

In psychological terms, ambition is your capacity to be energized, similar to a motive or a drive. You have the potential both to feel and to express ambition. The psychoanalyst Alfred Adler described it in his book *The Education of Children* as a natural desire to reach higher levels of completeness and fulfillment. He links ambition to the development of the striving for superiority which he believes is basic to all individuals.

Ambition Linked, Not Isolated

Linked! That may be the key for understanding ambition. It is linked to other aspects. Ambition does not stand alone, nor should it be an end in itself. It's like any of your desires—when they become the end, they dominate and destroy. The ambition of workaholics is their end—ambition for ambition's sake. However you define ambition, you will find that it is linked to your desires and goals.

Observe your interests. Have you ever felt so captured by a task or a project that you worked at it intensely? I know individuals who devote hours to their hobbies while neglecting other necessary duties. Ambition in a young person springs into action when some goal or aspiration becomes important. If ambition stands alone, it grows cold like a red-hot ember removed from the fire.

Furthermore, try describing your ambition in isolation. You connect it to some tangible expression. You can only observe ambition when it is expressed in actions, competitions, or projects. You experience it in accomplishments, vocations, and achievements. Whereas some find that failures discourage their ambition, others use setbacks as stepping-stones to success. Can you see yourself still working on a project that failed over and over again? Thomas Alva Edison failed one hundred times before he invented the light bulb. Some of us would have given up after the third attempt—three strikes and we're out—but not Edison. Each failure left him with a stronger drive to succeed. Edison's ambition was linked to persistence.

Ambition by itself, then, is neither good nor bad, but it can become one or the other. Think of your ambition as an appetite. Your appetite for eating isn't the problem, it's obesity or anorexia. The one is eating too much, the other is not eating enough to live. The solution for both is not to get rid of your eating. It is eating in moderation. The same is true with your sexual appetite or your need for power and authority. Both can be misused, which can result in painful relationships. Yet, both, like your ambition, can be experienced in ways that produce enduring and fulfilling relationships.

Ambition Needs a New Look

What is needed is a new look at ambition. Let us dust off some old definitions and clear up some current misperceptions. Can you openly support ambition as a healthy aspect of what it means to be human? Can you own your ambition as a part of your life, to be used creatively and not misused? You and I can recognize that it was not ambition that was blind in John Dean, as suggested by his title, *Blind Ambition*. Other factors were at fault. The needs of his personality and the temptations in his situation at that time blinded his vision to see where his ambition was moving him. For every John Dean there are people like Andrew Carnegie, who once bought the library of a financially troubled businessman and deeded it back to the man without his knowing who did it. Remember that the yardstick for measuring the rightness or wrongness of ambition is the rightness or wrongness of the achievement to which it is directed or the rightness or wrongness of the means used to accomplish that achievement. Not the fuel but how it is used is the problem.

What Awakens Ambition?

If you agree with me that ambition is present in every person as a possible potential, then ask the questions: What awakens ambition? What sets ambition in motion? If ambition does not stand alone, to what is it linked? I have one simple answer—"You name it!" The energy of ambition is no respecter of directions, goals, aspiration, things, or "whatever." Ambition can be awakened by almost anything. The focus of ambition is as varied as there are ambitious people. But whatever does attract you, one thing is certain: your ambition is influenced by the past, the present, and the future and, above all, by the natural process of maturation. The past pushes ambition into action. The present presses it into motion. The future pulls it into expression. And your maturation provides a process for its development. As I describe aspects related to each of these, think about what pushes or presses or pulls your ambition. My list is partial; your list will be much more personal.

The Push of the Past

The past is a very important part of your life. Former experiences and memories can shape your present aims and aspirations. Depending upon the meaning given to these past experiences or memories, your present strivings may be used either to duplicate a pleasant past or to protect you from an unpleasant past. I know individuals who were raised on a farm, left to make their living in the city, and later returned to live on a few rural acres in order to enjoy again the memory of their earlier years.

You may want to forget your past. The depression of the 1930s was not an easy time for many. Maybe you experienced those years. What impact did they have upon you? People who are unable to forget the insecurity and uncertainty of their past often become *conservers.* "Don't throw away anything" is their motto. They use items longer and are more inclined to repair them instead of replacing them with new. Others become *accumulators.* They attempt to replace the poverty of their past with abundance in the present. Their push is, "Enough is never enough." Still others are *protectors.* They hold on to what they acquire, fearful that they might not have it again if they use it.

Poverty is often thought of as the classical ambition starter. It does often awaken ambition. Two brothers where I live are changing the downtown section of a major city of my state. These forty-year-old millionaires began life in a poverty pocket of eastern Appalachia. They determined to get an education and eventually came to one of the state's law schools. As new lawyers they bought an old house and renovated it for resale. The rest is history. Today they own multimillion-dollar building complexes.

The environment of your early family can be another factor. Some psychologists believe that children sure of their mother's love tend to be successful. An article in *Psychology Today* (March 1983) titled "Sons and Mothers, the Making of Powerful Men," describes the mother-son relationships of Lyndon Baines Johnson, Douglas MacArthur, Franklin Delano Roosevelt, Harry Truman, and Frank Lloyd Wright. You can't argue that these men were not ambitious.

Johnson recalls in first grade choosing to recite a poem titled "I'd Rather Be Mama's Boy." Truman seldom let a week pass without calling or writing his mother; within thirty minutes of the Japanese surrender he was on the phone talking with her in Grandview, Missouri. Frank Lloyd Wright's mother (who never doubted that she was carrying a son) decided before his birth that he was to be an architect; she decorated his room with framed engravings of great cathedrals and gave him, as toys, all kinds of colored cardboard shapes and smooth maple blocks.

Past attitudes and atmospheres can be strong influences on the way you view yourself. The affirmations received, the encouragement experienced, the firmness of the guidance given—these experiences and others shape your personal image.

One aspect of self-image is the way you feel about your appearance. Take height for an example. There is what some call the Napoleonic complex, which assumes that short people are filled with ambition as a form of compensation. I have a friend who is barely 5 feet 5 inches tall. He admits that being short increased his ambition, but he is a big person in influence, talent, and drive. Shorter people do face challenges, especially in sports. When I played forward in college basketball games, six-three wasn't too short for that spot. I learned to watch out for opposing short players. They could take the ball out of my hands and be going the other direction before I could raise my arms over my head in despair. When that happened I felt a new surge of ambition (plus embarrassment).

These are a few ways you and I experience the push of the past. What out of your past sets ambition in motion for you? It may be something different from the things I have identified.

The Press of the Present

The "big three" pressures in today's culture are money, security, and status. These are sought after as ends as well as means to other ends. Who are the heroes in our society? Are they not frequently those who negotiate big contracts or achieve positions of prestige and status?

Notice the themes in American novels. Aleksandr Solzhenitsyn, the transplanted Russian novelist, has pointed out in one of his novels, *The First Circle,* that Western novels focus upon careers, money, and fame. For example, take the passion for money. Not many of us can view the film based upon F. Scott Fitzgerald's novel *The Great Gatsby* and not in some way be drawn by the wealth of silk shirts, expensive cars, and parties around beautiful backyard pools. How do you cut through the splendor? Do you recognize the thread of decay that eats away at the moral fibers of the very being of a person who dines daily at the table of opulence without giving to those who don't even have tables?

Maybe you feel pressures related to your salary. Salaries are often cited to draw attention to certain vocations or goals. A 1983 report stated that the college graduate earns $326,000 more over a working lifetime than the individual with only a high school diploma. Money gets further distorted in professional sports. The free agent is one form of a modern-day go-getter. Philadelphia pitcher Steve Carlton asked "only" that his 1983 salary be the highest given to a pitcher. The "only" meant $1.17 million. Sports fans spend billions to support team owners who give millions to pay adults who become the best players at their "play." I recognize that these are the exceptions. Furthermore, athletes are not the only ones caught. Many Americans are raised to get all they can. Competition is only one form of this type of thinking. We do need to keep in mind, however, that ambition directed toward financial fruits is a necessary fact of living. The issue again is not the wrongness of ambition but the distortion surrounding the gaining of wealth.

Security is another magnet that attracts ambition. The changes in our society make it more difficult for individuals to provide their own security nets beneath them. Many of you are seeking your security through the institutions where you work. Interest in seniority among union workers, in tenure among educators, and in pensions by most workers is a fairly recent expression of the natural desire for security. Contract negotiations become bogged down not so much on the wage issue but over the fringe benefits related to security. Job and retirement security is where the real emotion is invested.

Americans also use a lot of ambition to achieve status and prestige. This can take many forms. Job titles have proliferated in recent years. Everyone wants a title. In some corporations the title Junior Vice-President is used to satisfy the ambitious younger executives. The rank of professor is often sought by educators no matter how undistinguished their careers might be. Designer clothes and prestigious brand names lead the hit parade of status-conscious Americans.

As a parent I early faced the appealing advertisement of designer clothes. It's not the blouse or shirt most children desire. They are attracted to the animals or symbols sewn on the left-front pockets. Some of you have bought more alligators (on shirts) than all the zoos in America combined. My children also taught me that you don't wear new jeans before they are washed. I gave in on the outside. But can you

understand the battle I felt on the inside when as a boy I resisted washing a new pair of bib overalls? Secretly I never
wanted to wash them, so the newness would always be there.
Newness didn't come that often in a farm family of six boys.

There is no limit to status-focused ambition. The present
pressures for wealth, prestige, and security capture the ambition of many. What, in the present, pressures your ambition into high gear?

The Pull of the Future

The anticipation and the dreams of future achievements
and accomplishments are a powerful generator of ambition.
Take inventory on what makes you ambitious. How much of
your ambition is enticed by future possibilities? At a very
early age, children are motivated by the anticipation of some
future reward. Parents seek to stir up ambition in their children by offering future payoffs. I will never forget our Fri-
day trips to town as boys. My brothers and I were ambitious
on Fridays because as soon as we had the chores done we
knew we would each be going to town to get a nickel double-
decker ice-cream cone.

The pull of the future on our ambitions as children is just
as real when we are adults. This was my experience as a college junior. I was engaged to be married in August. June and
July were the only months I had to earn money before the
wedding. Talk about ambition! Those months took a long
time ending, but my weeks were filled with enthusiasm and
anticipation. I earned as much in those two months as I had
earned the three previous summer months. After twenty-five
years of marriage I still can recall the ambitions that flowed
in me as I was pulled by future desires.

Ambition is also activated in you by anticipating future opportunities. Benjamin Franklin felt that ambition flourished
in America because the opportunities were so many. People
were motivated by their dreams because they were attain-
able. Onward and upward was for a long time the prevailing

American spirit. America was founded by those who believed it to be the land of possibilities, open to all to go from log cabins to the White House. So fathers worked hard at the foundry precisely because they did not want their sons to be foundry workers. They sought to provide their sons opportunities to better themselves.

The development of future goals is another significant awakener of ambition. You can observe this fact in students who begin college with little concern for academics but with a large interest in social life. Their first-year academic achievements may be a disaster. Then they discover an interest that develops into a goal or a vocational direction. Suddenly ambition is sparked and flames into a discipline that ends up putting their name on the dean's list. The capacity of future goals to activate ambition can't be underestimated.

The Process of Maturation

More than past, present, or future aspects there is a common spark for all of us that sets our ambition in motion. That spark is the natural process of maturation. As a child you grew physically and matured emotionally. You also developed a growing potential to express ambition. You might compare it to your development of other natural drives. Your parents enjoyed a lot of satisfaction as they watched you strive for new accomplishments. The first time my son pulled himself up without help and stood alone remains as a special memory. I can still see him standing in his playpen. He certainly looked pleased with himself!

In your early childhood years the capacity for you to experience ambition increased with your physical and emotional development. As you matured you aspired to achieve the usual desires of a growing child. You see this in your own children as they reach for individual autonomy. The degree of ambition that you expressed in those early stages was determined by a variety of factors, but maturation sparked its possibility.

Ambition is a natural part of your life. It is neither inherently bad or good, right or wrong. The rightness or wrongness is determined by the goals toward which you direct your ambition. Ambition does not stand alone; you link it to desires and aspirations. Like any other energy it can be either your friend or your enemy. Which is it for you? I invite you to interact with me as I discuss these two possibilities. Take time to reflect upon your ambitions.

Part II

AMBITION AS ENEMY

Chapter 2

Demanding What Is Coming to You: Ambition Undisciplined

Father, give me the portion of goods that falleth
to me.

Luke 15:12

There is an interesting change in our society today. The
"spoiled child" is being replaced by the "hurried child." From
the 1940s to the early 1960s many parents were taught that
discipline would repress their children's creativity. Parents
read: "Allow your child freedom to express feelings." "Too
many restrictions limit a child's creativity." Consequently,
left without clear guidelines or firm boundaries, children in-
dulged in their most immature impulses. Many were given
freedom they were not ready to handle, power they did not
know how to control, and responsibilities they were not able
to carry out. These children often felt pressured to grow up
too quickly.

The concern of this chapter is the way patterns of ambition—both damaging ones and helpful ones—got started in
your life and, in turn, how you affect the flow of ambition in
the life of your children. In other words, both destructive
and creative ambitions do not just happen. They have a
growth history. I hope to describe ways both of these happen and what you can do to make ambition your children's
friend and not their enemy. The trend away from spoiled

children toward hurried children is the central concern of this chapter.

Shortened Childhoods in a Hurried World

In *The Hurried Child,* child psychologist David Elkind reports that he no longer sees spoiled children, but children who are thrust into adult roles too soon. He concludes, "Unlike the spoiled children who remain children too long, hurried children grow up too fast, pushed in their early years toward many different types of achievement and exposed to experiences that tax their adaptive capacity" (p. xii).

Elkind's sketch of hurried children may be new to you, but it is not without its ancient reflection. The Gospel of Luke tells the story of a young boy who wanted to grow up before he was ready. He was the second of two sons, a position that often produces accelerated ambition. The story begins with this younger son asking, "Father, give me the portion of goods that falleth to me" (Luke 15:12). The father divided the inheritance, and the son journeyed to a far country. He eventually lost his fortune because of undisciplined living. He wasn't ready for what he experienced. In the "far country" he was forced to take on responsibilities that he was not able to manage. He demanded what was coming to him before he was capable of handling his desires.

Have you watched that happen to children? They want adult responsibilities before they are ready. Some of that tendency is healthy. Children test their wings by taking on adultlike loads. However, when given too much responsibility too soon, children may feel overwhelmed. This is what Elkind says has happened to a large portion of today's troubled children. They are pushed to call forth ambitions before they possess the self-discipline to harness these energies. The result is predictable. To assume adult tasks too soon shortens childhood.

Some of you know what it means to have had a shortened

childhood. You were rushed through your early years by situations and demands over which you had no control. Part of the pressure came from a changing society. If you grew up in the 1960s, you experienced an atmosphere of rebellion. Maybe you rejected the work-ethic steps to success and were angered by a war judged by some to be unjust. You may have felt that there wasn't as much you could enthusiastically support as there was to oppose.

If you were a product of the 1970s, you were raised during a shift in the emphasis of ambition. Young people were less inclined to drop out of the mainstream of society. Like many you may have appeared apathetic, which led some to a form of self-gratification. This period is described as the age of narcissism, which means a preoccupation with oneself. The question was, "What's in it for me?" Ambition became self-oriented.

Maybe you were pushed toward adulthood by other factors, such as your family's drive for success. Parental expectations have a long shadow and are often felt very early in a child's life. Perhaps to be the best, to achieve, was the childhood motto given you. Others of you may have been faced in those formative years with the adult task of surviving through a divorce or the death of a parent. You had to grow up fast if you were going to make it at all. These kinds of experiences demand grown-up responses.

Hurried Through Maturation

What happens when you are hurried through your childhood years? For one thing, you experience conflicts in the various areas of your social, emotional, and physical growth. Conflict occurs because seldom do we mature in these areas at an equal rate. Advancements in nutrition and in health care have greatly accelerated physical maturation. Rapid physical development is especially evident in sports. Americans are running faster, jumping higher, and performing at record levels at earlier ages than ever before. Most Olympic swimmers are at their peak before they are accustomed to being teenagers.

That's some of the stress. Studies suggest that as the time clock of a child's physical development is accelerating, the child's emotional growth doesn't necessarily keep pace. Emotional maturity takes more time to develop than does physical maturity. Many children are expected to contain ten-gallon ambitions with pint-size emotional capacities. A thirteen-year-old girl may play tennis better than most adults, but she still has to deal with her thirteen-year-old emotions. Adult stress can be overwhelming.

Maybe you still remember the stress of your childhood. These memories don't fade quickly, especially when they left a profound impact upon you. Another reason is that most of the causes of those stresses are still present today. You continue to face them, but so do your children. Actually, growing up in the '80s bombards children with more information, experiences, and technology than many of us faced during our formative years. Stress-related problems, usually confined to adults, are developing in children at earlier ages. Pressure to assume adult maturity explains in large part why children are involved in delinquency, drugs, and school failures. Faced with adult tasks and tensions before they are prepared emotionally and psychologically, children feel bewildered and stressed. Even their capacity for ambition, which also needs time to develop, is placed under adult demands in order to cope with their hurried life.

Hurried by Cultural Influences

In addition to the uneven maturation demands that some of you felt, other influences that shaped your early life continue to confront children. These influences create further stress for children and demand from them a maturity that is often too advanced for their stage in life.

Rapid change is one influence that has become even more profound today. This is the Age of the Computer. The speed of life is being accelerated. Hand calculations that once took days to complete are done by computers in less than a minute. Computerized printing presses produce finished books of this size, bound and ready for shipping, at the rate of one hundred every minute. Home computer games are a lot faster than any games I played as a child. Do you find it hard to get children to sit long enough to set up a game like Monopoly, let alone play it? Sagging sales prompted the company to develop an electronic component that speeds up play.

If you and I are uncomfortable with the rapid assembly-line way of living, most children must feel confused. Change is the hallmark of their life; nothing seems permanent. New products become outdated within days of being placed on the market. Some experts claim knowledge doubles every ten years. Does that boggle your mind? It does mine! Then there is the unstable condition of today's family. By 1990 over 50 percent of all children will have divorced parents. Those children's whole supportive network has altered. These rapid changes push children to deal with more stress at a faster pace than they are ready to handle.

Educational trends are another strain you and your children face. Once you were told it was poor parenting to accelerate a child's learning. Not true today. Many of you feel the crunch to start your child's formal learning before kindergarten age. Head-start programs, prekindergarten schools, and home learning centers are top priority with young parents. More parents are putting the squeeze on school systems to offer advanced learning programs, increasing competition to win one of these spots.

In some school systems lack of funds results in overcrowded classrooms and inadequate facilities. Some children are promoted before they are ready. Others, with average ability but stressed by the pressure to advance, are labeled as learning disabled. Some even graduate with diplomas they find hard to read.

Your role as a parent is further complicated when educators urge you to create schools in your home. "Prepare your children for today's advances" is the appeal of one ad selling home curriculums for three- and four-year-olds. The issue is not should parents be teachers. You do more teaching as a parent than any other significant person in your child's life. But this teaching is informal, by example and by modeling daily living.

That's the pressure you face, if you are a parent, to formalize your parental role as a teacher. You may even feel derelict as a parent if you are not engaging your preschool child in formal home learning opportunities. The argument is to do all you can with these early years. But not all experts agree. Jean Piaget and Maria Montessori, two famous child educators, both recognized the stress and pressures that a formal approach to home training brings to preschoolers. Neither advocated formalizing the parent's teaching role. Children were viewed by them as needing time to be children.

Affluence is another shaper of ambition. Observe the young people around you. Most of them have more money than you did at their age. The abundance of luxuries, a mark of the '60s and the '70s, especially affects teenagers. Graham Blaine studied the hazards of overabundance. He believes that affluence "has affected the growing child by depriving him of the opportunity to meet a truly satisfying challenge" (p. 11). When you define maturity as the ability to postpone gratification, you can measure your own maturity by your capacity to postpone desired fulfillments. Ambition is nurtured by learning the rewards of waiting.

That's the issue! Many children don't have to wait. Luxuries abound! Bicycles, personal radios, private telephones, and automobiles are no longer the exception, even among middle-class youth. Now credit comes easy to many college students. Why? "The college market is a very desirable one," says Irvin Penner, president of the College Credit Card Corporation. Penner estimates that 5 million full-time college students have $600 million in disposable income. Ambition can get bored in the midst of easy luxury.

Like today's children, some of you were also shaped by *modern media.* Radios, books, movies, and television were an expected part of your life. The impact of these forms of communication upon you and your children is immeasurable. The world is immediately accessible through television. Your children see more on television than your grandparents ever saw in a lifetime. The technology of the media today forces children to deal with the realism of society's ills before they have mastered the tasks of childhood. As an adult you are expected to control your impulses and to take responsibility for your behavior. But you developed the base for these capacities during your childhood years. This took time and support, two ingredients often missing for today's children. Exposure to sexual behavior before children have the emotional maturity to handle that behavior can leave them feeling confused. They may be ready physically, but they are not ready spiritually. Hence, they arrive at premature "closure" on one of life's major decisions—choosing a mate—before they can fulfill the demands of intimacy. Then they lose heart and the "fuel of achievement" is spent.

Advertising produces another pressure on your children's ambition. Observe the appearances that advertisers promote. Preschool children are enticed to wear miniature versions of adult clothing. Try to put your child into a shirt or blouse that doesn't have a designer emblem. You end up feeling like a child abuser. Madison Avenue executives know how to get to your pocketbooks, and image is one of the ways. Brooke Shields was a preteen when she began to look and move like a young adult. The suggestions are numerous. Dress your children like adults, and they are more likely to imitate adult actions. Often they want to go where adults go, see what adults see, and do what adults do. Society may physically dress them like miniature adults on the outside, but they are still children on the inside, needing to sort through a childhood they are rapidly losing.

Competition is one more cultural influence. The crucial stage, according to child psychologist Erik Erikson, is the early school-age period. This is a vulnerable time for children as they attempt to establish some sense of competence. If they lack the skills of their peers, they feel inferior in competitive situations and may believe, Erikson says, that they are doomed to inadequacy. Ambition in its respectful form is quenched.

Competition is central in our society's obsession with sports. "Win at all costs" is the attitude. This is illustrated in a revealing article about tennis in *Sports Illustrated* titled "The Glitter Had Gone" (Nov. 8, 1982). Tennis prodigies, barely ten years old, are subjected to rigid practice schedules, hours of travel, and psychological pressures beyond their readiness. One potential star, Lori Kosten, after six years of this pressure, of throwing up from anxiety, and seeing a friend succumb to suicide, quit in the middle of a national girls' tournament. The sets were even. She was down 0–2 in the third set when she walked off the court and said to her dad, "Let's go." Lori barely touched a racket for the next two years. The pressure to be competitive can shorten childhood. This is ambition gone astray.

Concerned Parents with Misdirected Motives

The development of ambition is shaped not only by maturation and cultural influences but also by parental expectations and family values. As a parent you are deeply concerned about your child's well-being. However, sometimes that concern can get misdirected. You are stretched and stressed by the same pressures that hurry children. But there is a difference. Much of the pressure that your children experience comes from your stress. Elkind is candid when he writes, "We hurry children because stress induces us to put our own needs ahead of their needs" (p. 28). In attempting to give your children a head start in life you may urge them to take on physical, emotional, and social ambitions before they are prepared to handle them.

Furthermore, you may discover that your concern for your children is being distorted by pressures you feel. For example, you may find that a child has become a substitute for your own unfulfilled desires. Or you may discover that he or she is a symbol for your status. Or you may even learn how you expect your children to serve some of your adult needs. As a parent I know it is not easy to admit to these shortcomings. You may not even be comforted by the fact that many parents can identify with you. However, when you admit your particular misdirected concern for your child, you both will be the winners.

Substitutes for Self

In different ways all parents live out their ambitions through their children. This is a mutual experience in family relationships. Your children learn responsibility and self-respect when you are responsible and respected. In return you feel affirmed when your children do well in school or in community activities. Families are important. They link members together and provide children a resource to draw upon in developing their individuality. Most of the time this interdependence is helpful. Yet, there are those incidents in all families when distortions and stresses occur.

When your job becomes boring and stressful you are more tempted to turn to your children for self-fulfillment. Elkind found that parents tended to push their children into team sports at an earlier age when their own work provided little satisfaction.

Some parents turn to their children as a substitute to satisfy unfulfilled dreams. I read about one mother who had entered her daughter in sixty beauty contests before she was twelve years old. Fathers sometimes expect their sons to

achieve what they didn't. Barbara Bowman, a child development expert, describes parents who are so anxious that their
child might be left behind that there is almost a hysteria connected with it. In an article titled "Bringing Up Superbaby"
(*Newsweek*, March 28, 1983), she tells about a single mother
who works two jobs so she can provide her daughter devel-
opmental day care, educational toys, and swimming lessons.
The daughter is twenty-two months old! A child can feel
overwhelmed and vulnerable when expected to do too much
too soon.

Symbols of Self

Another way you may pressure your children is by expecting them to satisfy your need for recognition, a natural human desire. You experience self-affirmation when your child
is successful or "advanced" for his or her age. That's great!
Children need proud parents. However, if your children
sense in you that their achievements are only for you, they
may eventually give up or strive harder to assure continued
support. In the first case, ambition fades; in the second, the
child may become ambition-ridden.

Competition is one means for gaining prestige. Play in the
Joseph Kennedy family was designed to end in winning. Eu-
nice Kennedy Shriver once reported, "I was twenty-four before I knew I didn't have to win something every day" (Epstein, pp. 195-196). The drive to win in the three politically
minded Kennedy sons was reinforced by the words of their
dad, "In this family we want winners!" Ted Kennedy's natural desire to run for the office of President is further complicated in the wake of the death of two brothers with unfulfilled presidential goals.

Academic achievement is another favorite symbol by
which parents gain status from their children. Linda and
Bruce Hale have two sons. Their three-year-old was just able
to squeeze into the last opening in a prestigious Boston Montessori school at a cost of two thousand dollars a year.

"There's so much pressure to get into college," says thirty-eight-year-old Linda. "You have to start them young and push them on toward their goal. . . . I want to fill these little sponges as much as possible" (Bowman, "Bringing Up Superbaby," p. 62; used by permission). You need not question the basic goal to recognize that the eagerness of ambition can become misdirected.

Children pushed too fast may retreat into apathy as a means to resist more pressure. Tom, raised on a Kentucky farm, moved with his family to New York City. Oppressed by the dramatic change, and pushed by the faster urban pace, he retreated into his own world. Years later he recalls, "It took me ten months to recover. I heard my dad tell my mother, 'He wasn't lazy back home.' It wasn't laziness, it was my only means of protection. I needed time to regroup." Today Tom has a Ph.D. He concludes, "I always felt an ambition to go beyond my background, but I had to go at my pace."

Servants to Self

Maybe you find yourself wanting your children to serve your individual needs. In unhappy marriages and after a divorce or the death of a spouse, single parents, living alone, long for companionship. There is a lot of loneliness in being left to raise your children without the emotional support of a spouse. One widowed mother expected her ten-year-old son to go with her each week to the movies. This expectation continued even when the son became older and wanted time with his friends. Her remark to me was, "My husband and I enjoyed movies together every week without fail." She soon saw how she expected her son to serve this loss of companionship.

Have you ever wished your children could help you make a decision? For a twelve-year-old, preparing dinner may not be too ambitious a task, but deciding with which parent to spend Christmas or Easter is another matter.

Children are often asked to become confidants. They serve as sympathetic listeners, hearing complaints and learning about conflicts that are more than they can handle. This forces them to function at an interpersonal level for which they are not emotionally prepared. As one young adult told me, "When I was six my dad told me things about Mom to get me to like him more than her. And my mom told me things to gain my support for her."

Sometimes you may expect your child to accept behaviors that most adults would frown upon. Elkind describes a father who deserted his wife and two children. He moved into the home of his new girlfriend and invited his children to spend some time with them. He did not hide his affection for the woman or the fact that they were sleeping together. He expected his children to accept his new living arrangement, which they were unprepared to understand, let alone condone. The illustrations of parents with misdirected concerns are many. The results are the same—children forced to deal with adult issues while still children.

Suggestions for Helping Hurried Children

If you are a parent, one thing I know, you care about your children. You are interested in how they grow up, how they are doing in school, and how they get along with others. You are especially concerned that they learn right from wrong, develop faith in God, and handle the pressure to grow up too fast. Here are some suggestions for helping children to be less hurried.

Live Today, Today

One of the best ways you can support your child is for you to live each day, today. When you concentrate on the here and now, without worrying about yesterday or tomorrow, your children will do likewise. Jesus taught this. He said:

Take no thought for your life, what ye shall eat, or what ye shall drink. . . . Behold the fowls of the air: for they sow not, neither do they reap . . . ; yet your heavenly Father feedeth them. Are ye not much better than they? Which of you by taking thought can add one cubit unto his stature? . . . For your heavenly Father knoweth that ye have need of all these things. But seek ye first the kingdom of God, and his righteousness; and all these things shall be added unto you. Take therefore no thought for the morrow: for the morrow shall take thought for the things of itself. Sufficient unto the day is the evil thereof. (Matt. 6:25-27, 32-34)

This is not a license for irresponsible living but a prescription for peace in the here and now. You and I can become so anxious about tomorrow that we miss the pleasures of today.

I am still learning to live today, today. Each day I try to pause intentionally for a moment of rest and quiet enjoyment of something present. Many times it's to watch a sunrise through my living room window or to ponder quietly the blessings of my life or to marvel at the vastness of a starry summer night or to listen to the steady sound of a spring rain. These experiences help me to live in the present. They become moments of devotion that move me to worship God. I do not restrict these "pauses for refreshment" by time or content. Some days I take only a few minutes; other days I enjoy a much longer time. Sharing these present experiences with your children will help them live more peacefully. Children like to live in the present, and they know when you are with them. If you are a working mother, enjoy moments with your child free of your regrets for times not there or separations yet to come. If you are a busy father, capture opportunities to be present with your child free of judging yourself for the amount of time you give. The length of each contact is not as important as the meaning of your presence.

Invest Time for Future Dividends

This suggestion builds upon the previous one. Hurried children need regular unhurried time. John and Charles Wesley, founders of Methodism, were raised in a family of eleven children. Mrs. Wesley spent individual time each week with each child. She wrote, "To inform their understanding is a work of time, and must, with children, proceed by slow degrees as they are able to bear it" (William Orr, *Bible Hints on Rearing Children,* pp. 18-19; Scripture Press, 1955).

A friend told me how he plans regular time with his three growing children. They may go out together for ice cream or to a park or on a hike. One summer he took each child separately on a camping trip. He used one weekend each month. On these occasions his children are the most open to express their thoughts and feelings. My wife and I found traveling in the car to be choice opportunities for conversations with our children. We learned that the amount of time together needed to be sufficient for all of us to make contact. Yet the regularity of being together was more important than the length of these times.

James Dobson writes (p. 55), "It takes time . . . to fly kites and play punch ball and put together jigsaw puzzles. It takes time to listen, once more, to the skinned-knee episode and talk about the bird with the broken wing. These are the building blocks of esteem, held together with the mortar of love." Think of those times with your children as investments for future dividends. Allow yourself the right to enjoy childhood with your child. You both deserve to play, and play is nature's way of dealing with stress.

Stay in Step with Your Child's Pace

This is a biblical principle. Isaiah 28:10 describes its process: "For precept must be upon precept . . . ; line upon line . . . ; here a little, and there a little." Children have an inner timetable that governs their growth pace. You can overload their emotional circuits with too many "precepts" and "lines" too soon. Just as you space out the finishing coats of lacquer on a fine piece of antique furniture, you must allow children time to absorb each stage of their growth process. This is not always easy in a society that puts a premium on growing up fast. Keeping pace is further complicated when you have more than one child. No two children develop at the same pace. Neither do children move through each stage in the same manner. Nor is a child's perceptions the same throughout his or her life. Young children tend to blame themselves when they are stressed. Teenagers tend to blame their parents. In each stage you can help by knowing the pace of your child.

One way you can stay in step with your child is through listening. Children need to feel they are heard. As you know so well, parents can miss hearing the voices of their children in the rush of life. In Thornton Wilder's play *Our Town,* there is a scene in which Emily says to her mother, "Listen to me, look at me." In many ways children tell their parents where they are in their journey toward maturity. I will never forget the evening my son called me aside and said, "Dad, can I talk with you? You don't need to decide anything. I only need you to listen to what I'm thinking about doing." By my son's actions and words he was telling me the level of his maturity and inviting me to respond to him with a parental role that was complementary. That evening my son helped me become more mature as a parent.

As your children grow they need you to adjust your parental style. Some parents get into binds with their teenagers because they haven't changed their style of parenting for ten years. You will stay in step with your children's pace when you consider their present age, their particular stress, and their immediate situation.

Give Your Child Positive Mottoes

The role of mottoes in our lives was introduced to me by David Seamands. In his book *Putting Away Childish Things,* Seamands writes about childhood mottoes that haunt adults. He tells the story of a pastor who struggled many years as an up-and-down Christian—successful outwardly but like a yo-yo inwardly. For years he bounced between spiritual highs and lows. Then, he reports (p. 30), "There came to me a flash of insight from the Holy Spirit. I suddenly realized that my life was not really being ruled by love for God and for other people. Instead, for the past forty-nine years a little childhood motto instilled in me by my parents had really been running my life." The motto was "Measure up!"

You and I know (as he did) that his parents didn't intend to give him this impression. But as a child he came to hear, "Sure, we love you, but we would love you more if only you would measure up!" Motto-building may be a new term, but that's what parents do. Your words and outlook shape your child's attitude and life mottoes. Negative mottoes may read like these: "What's wrong now?" "How stupid of you!" "You messed up again!" "You never get it right!" "Big boys don't cry!" "What's the use!"

Many of you can add to that negative list. But positive mottoes are more enjoyable to read and much more satisfying to give. I heard a delightful motto-building story from a young woman. She told me how her ambition was awakened when she brought home a picture she had drawn in the third grade. Her mother looked at it, gave her a hug, and said, "You know, something good is happening in you!" I would like to give that motto to any child, wouldn't you? Here are some more mottoes that are fun to give: "You wear well!" "Hey, you're special!" "You can do it!" "You're A-OK!" "You're somebody!" Add your mottoes to this list. Better yet, give one away today, "You'll like it!"

You and I can't change the basic thrust of our society for which hurrying is the accepted and valued way of life. We can't eliminate the pressures of impatience that push children to understand beyond their limits of understanding or to decide beyond their capacity to make decisions. At the same time children need responsibilities. They need to be given opportunities that are not totally free of risks. But they also need buffers from the abuses of hurrying. I liken this tension to football. If you never hand the ball to your children, it's true, they won't fumble, but neither will they ever know the satisfaction of scoring a touchdown. But when you do give them the ball, don't send them around right end while all the blockers are going to the left. They need protection from catastrophes too.

Being ambitious in the ways I have just suggested turns it into a friendly force instead of the enemy that hurrying your child makes of ambition. Such aspiration to enable your child to become himself or herself at the pace of God's creative "time clock" is God's image in the child and will bring you serenity, not just pride; and genuine satisfaction, not just vanity. You deserve serenity and satisfaction!

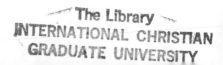

Chapter 3

Building Your Barns Bigger:
Ambition Self-directed

Soul, thou hast much goods laid up for many
years; take thine ease; eat, drink, and be merry.
Luke 12:19

Ambition as an enemy is never more destructive than
when you lavish it upon your own self. Ambition for the sake
of ambition soon becomes a self-serving passion. This passion is felt on two fronts. Individuals may become vain with
an excessive love for themselves. They are the "center attrac-
tion" of their world. Or the world becomes an obstacle to be
conquered. They disregard other people in their quest for
self-satisfaction.

Christopher Lasch, a cultural historian, wrote, "After the
political turmoil of the sixties, Americans have retreated to
purely personal preoccupations" (p. 4). He observes that
Americans, in considerable numbers, give little energy to improving life in general. The "in thing" is self-improvement.
To live for yourself is the prevailing passion.

The "Foolishness" of Self-service

Self-directed ambition, however, isn't new. Service for the
sake of self is as ancient as Adam and Eve in the Garden of
Eden. Actually, they were the first to become swept off their
feet with their own image in the pool of self-reflection. They
wanted to be king of the hill or "in the garden" right from

the start. It appears that the desire to build our barns bigger
is one hazard of being human.

What happens to you or to me when our ambition becomes self-directed? Jesus tells us what happened to one
man. With clear and candid words he told the story of a
wealthy farmer whose land "brought forth plentifully." To
accommodate the record harvest he built bigger barns. When
the harvest was in and the barns were full he said to himself,
"Soul, thou hast much goods laid up for many years; take
thine ease; eat, drink, and be merry" (Luke 12:19). He
sounded like one who had found the good life. But Jesus
called him foolish. You and I might call him selfish.

Selfish not because he was wealthy. Jesus never made a
blanket indictment of wealth. Rather, he condemned the
misuse of wealth and cautioned us about the temptations that
often come with wealth—covetousness being first on the list.

Selfish not because the man was successful. Success is not
sin. I would not be surprised to learn that this man was highly
respected in his community; maybe a leader on the town
council or on the school board or even in his church. His
family was probably well respected in the local community.
He could be compared to any of today's self-made millionaires. Success is not in itself either foolish or the sign of selfishness.

Neither is producing record harvests or building new
barns to store the abundance inherently wrong. Here is the
fly in the ointment. When our ambition becomes self-directed, our life can become distorted! Priorities get confused. We can develop a very narrow vision. That's the ab-
surdity of this man's actions. He let his living get out of
balance. He failed to keep his life in its proper perspective.
The relationships between his physical life and his spiritual
life, between his human existence and his ultimate destiny,
became confused. As a result, he disregarded some basic relationships that are still important for us to maintain

today. When they are out of balance, our ambition can become more like an enemy than a friend.

The Relationship Between the Means and the End

You and I are created to labor, but not to worship the
fruits of our labors. Genesis 2:15 tells us that God created
Adam to care for the Garden of Eden. He was to participate
actively in creating. And so are we! But Adam was not to
worship what he created. And neither are we! This was the
failure of the man in the story Jesus told. He failed to keep
the means of his existence separated from the end of his existence. The structures that maintained his life became the
destiny of his life. His labors produced abundance, and he
came to worship the abundance. This resulted in the fullness
of his life becoming dependent upon the fullness of his
barns. That, Jesus said, is always foolish. The issue is not
whether there is more virtue in poverty than in wealth. Jesus teaches in this account that you and I must not let the
fruits of our labors, the results of the means, swallow up the
purpose of our very life itself—the end of our reason for being. He shows that self-directed ambition will narrow our
life. He doesn't question our need to make a living, or ne-
gate the possibility that our living may become quite successful. But Jesus cautions you and me not to lose our life in the
worship of the living we make.

The Relationship Between the Created and the Creator

We are created in the image of God, but we are not to act
as if we are God. Again, this story illustrates how self-directed ambition can cause us to behave like God. Notice the
rich man's words. His ambition was oriented toward his self-
glorification. He said, "My barns, my fruits, my soul, I have
things under my control; so take thine ease, eat, drink, and
be merry."

Does this man sound like anyone you know? Self-cen-
tered people often act as if everything turns around them. To

some degree all of us struggle with this human temptation. After all, there is dignity in being human, and it is important to affirm our humanness. We are created in God's image and reflect that image. The wrong is setting God aside and replacing him with ourselves or, worse, living as if God wasn't needed. The man in the story stopped living as the one who was the creature and began to live as if he were the Creator. You and I can affirm that we are created in the likeness of God, but Jesus said it is folly to forget our dependency upon God.

The Relationship Between the Individual and the Community

We are created as individuals, but we are not islands unto ourselves. We do possess a degree of self-rule, but we are not free from being our brother's or sister's keeper. The man in the story forgot his interdependence with others. He said "I" and "my" so often he lost the capacity to say "we" and "our." He failed to realize that wealth always comes as a result of the commonwealth.

Self-directed ambition can lead us down the same path. When we stop looking beyond ourselves, our world can become very small. We see this in self-centered individuals. They tend to act as though everything belongs exclusively to themselves. They live as if they have the full monopoly of their belongings and the freedom to use them only for their own pleasure and enjoyment. Life is no longer in balance for people who behave this way because they fail to realize the relatedness of their life to others. Let's look again at the story Jesus told. The man began to talk as though he unfolded the seasons and provided the soil. He forgot that he was enjoying the labors of those who cleared the land and tamed the wilderness. He began to act as if he controlled the rising and the setting of the sun. He lived as though he could go it alone, failing to recognize his dependence upon others and upon his Creator. That's the ultimate foolishness of self-service. When we begin to build our barns bigger for the sake of bigger barns, it is like being eaten by our own consumption. Self-directed ambition can become self-destructive.

When the Consumer Is Eaten Alive

The danger of self-directed ambition is that as consumers we may be consumed—eaten alive! The energy of our ambition can become addicting. What happens when we see this kind of ambition in others? We stay clear. Nobody wants to get scorched by the intensity of another's heated desires. This kind of all-consuming ambition makes us cautious about ambition. Many people have admitted to me that the word "ambition" projects a negative image. Some even view ambition as an enemy "to watch out for," an enemy to be conquered, rather than as a friend to be embraced. "If you feel the stirrings of ambition, it is best to keep them hidden" is their advice. Have you known people who were uncomfortable to be described as ambitious? To them it means being so self-centered that one is never satisfied, or that one is in danger of becoming an "ambition-aholic." "Success begets success," they say, "but ambition begets distrust."

The fear of ambition as an enemy is not without support. American novels describe ambitious characters who are not the ones we would think well of, and certainly not those we copy. Men are pictured as ruthless, insensitive, and without depth of character. Women are likely to be described as shrewd, manipulative, and seductive. The fact is that when we focus our ambition upon ourselves it can consume us or blind us with self-glory.

Consumptive Ambition

Our society is not without its consumers who get eaten alive by their appetite during the act of consuming. In an interesting book *Who Gets Ahead?* Christopher Jencks observes how progress in America is the most important product. The meaning of life tends to be reduced to unending change. Progress becomes the goal. Bigger and better, more and more, faster and faster, are the ends. When we get caught up in this whirl of things, we have to go with the tide or ride the wave of the future.

Victor Gielisse is the executive chef of the Westin Oaks Hotel in Houston's upbeat Galleria Mall. He is one of the best, with a gold medal to prove it. He is also an example of one who feels wasted by his ambition. Speaking about a culinary competition he won, he recalls, "I get tense; I am shaking like a leaf. Then I win a gold medal, and I feel this emptiness inside, I'm thinking what's next?" ("Where Competition Seasons," *ComAir Magazine,* November 1982, p. 71; reprinted courtesy *United* Magazine, carried aboard United Airlines. © 1982. East/West Network, Publisher.) Have you ever felt that way when caught in a spiral of ambition of the self-directed kind? Achieving becomes an all-devouring passion. Like a drink of salt water, each achievement leaves you thirsty for another. You may feel edgy with your successes, longing to push on to something else. What keeps you going is the "doing," not the "ending."

Maybe you are one who feels at a loss without something to do. Retirement is not in your vocabulary, nor relaxation in your experience. You are uncomfortable with too much time. Epstein describes a retired dry-cleaning chain owner who sold his eight stores for in excess of half a million dollars. He continued to rise each day at the same six-o'clock hour, dress in his suit, and drive to the same restaurant. As he left, he wondered, "How am I going to get through this day?" (*Ambition,* pp. 219–220).

Consumptive ambition is like an ulcer; it eats away at the meaning of life. Our appetites become linked to a never-ending merry-go-round of cravings for wealth, prestige, or power.

Self-glory Ambition

Christopher Lasch sees a new trend toward self-glory in our society. People who are caught up by this trend seem to live only for "what's in it for me?" Their cravings have no limits and they are bent on immediate gratification. Lasch contends that America is fast becoming a narcissistic, self-love culture, haunted not by guilt but by anxiety.

You can appreciate what Lasch is saying by recalling the early Greek myth about a handsome young hunter named Narcissus, whose self-love was so intense he could not love anybody but himself. One day he knelt by a crystal-clear pool and saw his reflection for the first time. Since he was unable to leave the image in the pool, his body eventually wasted away with grief and longing until his remains were nowhere to be found. Only a wax-white flower with a purple heart stood in the place where he had knelt. Grieving maidens who came looking for the young hunter named the flower Narcissus.

This myth is not as ancient as you might think. There is a little narcissism in all of us. You may know persons who desire not so much to be respected as to be admired. They crave glamour and want to be envied instead of commended. The fact that they have made it matters most, and their self-glory becomes grandiose. The line between a healthy appreciation for yourself and self-glory can become very narrow.

Ambition as self-glory is described by psychologist Bruce Narramore as an "inordinate attention to one's self and the gratification of his or her needs and wishes" ("Biblical Self-esteem in an Age of Narcissism," *The Asbury Seminarian*, Winter 1982, p. 6; used by permission).

> These persons become oriented to receive rather than to give, to satisfy their needs rather than another's, to be immediately gratified rather than

wait, and to use people rather than become mutually close. But above all, they develop a poverty of inner life, a sense of emptiness, a void that
the narcissistic person tries to fill by a round of activities, by calling attention to himself or herself,
or by using others to gratify his or her needs and
wishes. (Ibid., p. 7)

Grandiose ambition can really be destructive in a marriage. When one spouse becomes guided by the "what's in it
for me" attitude, both spouses can be very self-serving.
David Seamands, in his helpful book *Problem Solving in the
Christian Family*, calls this the "I-Me weed" in the "garden
of Marriage" (p. 65). This "weed," says Seamands, grows to
enormous height, until nothing else can be seen in the garden. The self-directed attitude of the earlier immature child
never changes to the other-directed attitude of the mature
adult. When this is found in a marriage relationship, one or
both spouses take from each other with little giving in return. Intimacy, companionship, friendship, and support are
seldom mutually shared. The wife of a graduate student once
said to me, "I feel like my interests are of no importance. He
expects me to maintain the home, care for our three children, and work my job, while he buries his head in his studies so he can be a straight-A student. He doesn't want a wife
and family, what he wants is a hired servant." As seen in this
student, ambition channeled toward oneself can become a
superficial self-glory of one's reflection.

Playing King of the Hill for Keeps

Do you remember as a child playing king of the hill? I was
raised in a family of six boys. Because of the death of a sister just before I was born there was a gap between the three
oldest and the three youngest. I was the oldest of the last
three. Consequently, I was closer to my younger brothers.

One of our favorite games was king of the hill. If we couldn't find a hill large enough, we would make one. Since we lived on a farm we often used a haystack (much to my dad's frustration). In the winter it might be a snowbank. And more frequently than our mother ever knew it was our beds.

The goal of the game was simply to remain on top of the hill—the king! The ambition of the younger ones was to unseat the oldest. And the oldest felt the frantic necessity to remain number one. I have good memories of wrestling with my brothers as we tumbled down the side of one of those haystacks. It was all fun and games, most of the time. Occasionally, it heated up and became a serious challenge for the oldest to remain on top. As the oldest player I later came to understand the power struggle between older and younger brothers and sisters. There was some value in that game for us. It relieved the natural competitiveness of three healthy, active boys.

Adults play this game—king of the hill. But now the hills are positions, prestige, and power. Nor is the game played merely for fun, it's for keeps! The stakes are higher. The tumbles are more painful. The results ripple throughout our vocational life. The price of playing can become never-ending.

Self-directed ambition can take many forms for its expression. One form is when we are consumed, never satisfied, or when we are blinded by a grandiose self-image. These expressions of ambition are damaging to us personally. On the other hand, self-directed ambition can become destructive to others. To gain the upper hand as a child playing with other children on a haystack is quite different from climbing the corporate ladder for keeps as adults. Now ambition can become destructively competitive and excessively exploitive.

Competitive Ambition

Competition is a part of life. Ambition in a child is awakened and developed through competition. In many appropriate ways it is positive and valuable. Competition between siblings can awaken ambition. Brothers and sisters find comparisons and challenges between them to be motivators for achievements they might otherwise never have achieved. Yet competition can become quickly destructive. I continue to be surprised by how responsible adults involved in the political process can become irresponsible under the pressure of an election. Watergate will long stand as a reminder of one result of this change.

Again, competition is the key. When we view others as rivals they become obstacles to be conquered. It's a win-lose mentality. There is only one goal—"win at any cost." Competitive ambition is consumptive ambition turned onto others.

The title of John Dean's book *Blind Ambition* is aptly chosen. He describes his involvement in the Watergate scandal as that of being caught in the aspirations of a strong competitive motivation. Dean was in love with his "on the Hill" position. The ambition that motivated him to his position became self-oriented. The principle of "win at all costs" was not offset by other principles, such as personal integrity, ethical commitment, and public confidence. John Dean's ambition became a competitive force that could see only two options, win or lose. He determined to win.

Competitive ambition changes the way we order our lives. Whereas once our spirit of self-improvement would have condemned indulgence, now we are motivated by a spirit of survival at any cost. Whereas once we measured wealth by its contribution to the general good and to the happiness of future generations, now we value it only for what it will provide us. Whereas once we evaluated achievements against the ideals of discipline and self-denial, now we compare them with the achievements of others.

Wealth loses its moral moorings and becomes what someone called "a white heat of desire for money." Success forgets social concerns and becomes victory over one's competitors. Authority loses its ethical standards and self-restrained guidelines and becomes a license for self-indulgence. When our ambition is linked with competition for the purpose of serving only ourselves, we can become exploitive of others.

Exploitive Ambition

Exploitation is as ancient as human beings. Adam and Eve were exploited by the serpent. And King David succumbed to his desire for Uriah's beautiful wife, Bathsheba, when he manipulated Uriah into the most dangerous position in the battle, where he was killed. Exploitive ambition dulls our sensitivity to the value of others. When we play for keeps, we may end up using people and things for what we can gain from them.

Exploitive ambition is universal. In his book about modern man, *Man, the Manipulator,* Everett Shostrom defines a manipulator as a person who exploits, uses, and controls others as "things" in self-defeating ways. Watch those who manipulate. They use techniques and maneuvers to influence others. They focus so much on winning or competing that everybody but the game is missed. Have you noticed how they seek to be in control, concealing motives, feelings, and attitudes? Manipulators are skeptical, distrusting others and ultimately even themselves. Persons are used as means and not related to as human beings.

Let us admit, manipulation is all too common. We all do some of it. Actually, some manipulation seems inevitable in the marketplace of making a living. But that's the danger. We can grow accustomed to it. As I am describing it here, however, manipulation that becomes exploitive is designed solely for self-advantage. People are used. Real feelings and self-directed schemes are concealed and cloaked. A manipulative person makes subtle plans that may not even be obvious to himself or herself.

Like any ambition that is directed toward personal gain, manipulation not only hurts others, it also hurts the one doing the exploiting. When you or I treat others as "things," we not only dehumanize them, we also deface our own humanness. Exploitive ambition will ultimately leave us unable to enjoy our gains or to use our knowledge or to expand our sense of growth.

Ways to Reduce Barn-building

Have you gotten hooked on building your barns bigger? Do you at times feel consumed by your appetite for more? Maybe you are tired of playing king of the hill. Your ambition has enabled you to achieve, but you find your achievements leave you feeling inwardly unfulfilled. Here are two suggestions, or at least reminders, for reducing barn-building: build more spirituality and simplicity into your life.

Building Spirituality

Spirituality is the expression of a life lived in relationship to God. I do not mean knowing God in the abstract or as one to be feared, obeyed, or revered. Spirituality is a relationship where God is present not on the edges of your life but at the center of your experience. Brother Lawrence calls this "practicing the presence of God" and describes it in simple but inspiring words: "The time of business does not with me differ from the time of prayer; and in the noise and clatter of my kitchen, while several persons are at the same time calling for different things, I possess God in as great tranquility as if I were upon my knees at the blessed sacrament" (*The Practice of the Presence of God*, pp. 198–199; Judson Press, n.d.). This is knowing God in the everyday schedule of your life. What I am suggesting is that in an intentional way you should bring God into each activity.

Prayer is one of the keys to practicing the presence of God. Paul urged, "Pray without ceasing" (I Thess. 5:17). Have you wondered how you could get anything done if all you did was pray—that is, pray as most of us think of praying? Paul is describing prayer as an attitude, not only as an act. Live every day prayerfully! That's a far cry from the way most of us struggle through a day. Make these resolutions:

1. Consciously express a silent prayer for every person you meet today. You may meet them on the street, in an office, at a meeting; it doesn't matter where. Pray for them.
2. Pray over your decisions, your needs, and your desires. Prayer connects you into God's great supply of support.
3. Pray about your next purchases. Who doesn't need assistance with a pocketful of credit cards! You can't face the appeal for the bigger and better alone.

A couple told me they had accumulated twenty-three credit cards. They destroyed twenty-two, and in six months they were out of debt. Today they pray carefully about major purchases. They also wait at least a week to determine whether the purchase is right for them. This is one way to help yourself end impulse buying.

Another important way to deepen your spirituality is to participate in *monetary giving.* Some call it tithing, others proportionate giving. Will you have more money when you tithe? No! Technically, you have less—the amount you give. What you acquire is a new understanding of stewardship. You generally become more responsible with your earnings when you establish a regular commitment to give. Your attitude is the issue. There's a deep sense of joy in regularly sharing God's goodness. You give for "God's sake," not yours.

Spirituality is also developed by stressing the *quality of your life* above the quantity of your life. This is a paradox.

You increase your quality of life when you decrease your material desire. Listen to the words of one who practiced this paradox, John of the Cross: "Let your soul turn always not to desire the more, but the less" (quoted in Goldian VandenBroeck, ed., *Less Is More*, p. 26; Harper & Row, 1978). Richard Byrd wrote in his journal after months alone in the barren Arctic: "I am learning . . . that a man can live profoundly without masses of things" (*Alone*, p. 19; G. P. Putnam's Sons, 1938). That is not an easy lesson to learn. You will notice how you are constantly being urged to own rather than to be. Resist that urge by developing close friendships rather than acquiring things. Spend evenings together with those friends in conversation and fellowship. These times will become far more fulfilling than all the commercial entertainment your plastic cards will buy. Be creative! Plan evenings to build quality into your life, like listening to music, visiting art museums, or reading a good book. Watch for activities in your community that are free to the public or cost very little. On a visit to Washington, D.C., our family took a picnic lunch to the capitol lawn and heard a free concert by the Washington National Symphony. This was a highlight of our vacation.

Building Simplicity

To live simply is easier said than done. Entire books have been written on Christian simplicity. Richard Foster states, "Simplicity is both a grace and a discipline" (*Freedom of Simplicity*, p. 6). Simplicity is a grace because you receive it from God. You can't get it through your own strength or willpower. Yet discipline is demanded because you are called to cultivate consciously a life of moderation. Here are some suggestions on simplicity I found in Richard Foster's book. They are not meant to be rules but, rather, suggestions to be tried.

1. *Consciously agree as a family that you are going to resist the drive always to acquire more.* Make this a family conference issue. Talk about the role of advertising. Point out commercials that misrepresent or at best appeal to only the emotions. Play a game with your children. Have them keep a tally

of the ads that appeal to people's need for status and prestige.

2. *Put some action to your concerns.* Resist the urge to buy the "latest" and the "newest." Write the networks and companies producing commercials that misrepresent, informing them of your boycott of their products. Reject any junk mail you can. Remember, nothing is free! All of us would benefit if product costs were reduced by the cost of these contests.

3. *Consider cooperative buying and sharing.* Families in the same neighborhood can join in the purchase of items that are used only a few times a year. Why not purchase cooperatively Rototillers, garden tractors, chain saws, battery chargers? Some of these, like a battery charger, are rarely needed, but when they are you can save a service call. Car pooling and exchange baby-sitting make everybody a winner. What item do you want that could be bought cooperatively? Find a neighbor or a friend to join you in that purchase.

4. *Be aware of greed disguised as need.* I learned a lesson (actually I'm still learning it) from a beautiful lady in her seventies named Precious. She told me once, "The Lord always meets my needs. I have few needs, but a lot of wants." Do you fit that description? I do! "Buyer, beware of yourself!" A bargain is not a bargain unless you need it, can afford it, and plan to buy that item in the near future. You and I fool ourselves by calling it need. If you are like most people, you come away from bargain sales with items that you would never miss if you didn't have them.

5. *Seek moderation in all things.* Bigger and better is not necessarily best. Recreation is an example. You don't need the most expensive equipment to participate in physical exercise. Walking, jogging, and swimming are among the best forms of exercise and require a minimum of equipment. Make your recreation healthy, happy, and as gadget free as possible. When our children were younger we enjoyed riding our bicycles together or taking a walk. One evening I suggested we take our dishes of ice cream with us as we

walked. My children still enjoy a good laugh over us walking down the street with ice cream in a bowl rather than a cone. I also recall Sunday afternoon walks across fields or in wooded areas not far from where we lived.

Be ambitious for such simplicity, and you will find ambition to be your friend. Think seriously about what it is you are really acquiring in your climb to the top. Are you gaining things or a quality of life? The fruits of the Spirit are not push, drive, climb, acquire, and trample. The list includes love, joy, peace, long-suffering, gentleness, and goodness (Gal. 5:22–23). Be jealous for a quality of life that is not dependent upon the quantity of things. Your ambition is only as virtuous as the means it uses and the causes to which it is given. Use it for self-service, and it turns on you like an enemy. Direct it to build spirituality and simplicity, and your ambition will always be your friend.

Chapter 4

Desiring Your Camelot: Ambition Misdirected

> Grant unto us that we may sit, one on thy right hand, and the other on thy left.
>
> *Mark 10:37*

Are you acquainted with the phrase "upward mobility"? Most of us have experienced its pervasive drive. Upward mobility tries to sell you the bill of goods that the only way to go is up, that bigger is better. If you work hard and long, you can achieve the good life—even better than your parents. Sound familiar? Many of us in mid-life have tried to pass this attitude along to our children. Some of us have not succeeded. Our sons or daughters—or at least one of them—chose *not* to climb the ladder we held out to them.

Some parents find this hard to understand. Especially since ladder-climbing is rooted in American history. Many of the early settlers who came to America were manual laborers. They fled the hardships of poverty in the homeland with the hope of finding a better life in the New World. No one called it upward mobility then, but the desire to better oneself, and for parents to leave their children better off, was just as strong.

The "Drivenness" of Upward Mobility

Maybe the allure of upward mobility continues to capture a large share of your energies. Today's advanced technology and the abundance of affluence can shape all of us. As I was writing this chapter I tried a word processing system. The speed of this new way of making words is fascinating. I began to think, How can I keep up with society if I don't have a home computer? Our very sense of vitality seems dependent upon being part of the upward pull. Any of us can get caught in this type of drivenness. The two sons of Zebedee did.

Misdirected Ambitions

James and John were two of the disciples closest to Jesus. William Barclay titles their design to pull rank "The Request of Ambition" (*The Gospel of Mark,* rev. ed., p. 253; Westminster Press, 1975). The situation reads like a modern novel (Mark 10:35–37). Here are two small-town boys on their way up, excited by the chance to make it really big. They had seen and tasted with Jesus experiences that a lifetime on a fishing boat could never match.

Talk about go-getters! Grass wasn't going to grow under their feet. Their ambition was directed toward the highest positions. I wonder how long they talked about their desires before going to Jesus? Maybe they felt like some of us in similar situations. Here was their opportunity to get out of the fishing business. Never again would they anchor those fishing boats with little to show for their efforts.

You may remember the Broadway musical *Camelot.* In this mystical kingdom everything has to be perfect all year. It can't be too hot, and there is a legal limit on snow. Winter is forbidden until December, and summer lingers through September. Even the rain, by the king's decree, can't fall until after sundown. Like many of us these two sons of Zebedee were looking for their Camelot. Jesus talked as though a change was in the making. He had been telling them about coming kingdoms and performing marvelous acts of healing. Something must be in the air! And they wanted to be in on it. So they decided to strike while the iron was hot.

Mark indicated that they first tried to commit Jesus to their request before they told him what they wanted. That's a symptom to be noticed. It was a bold request. "Master, we would that thou shouldest do for us whatsoever we shall desire" (Mark 10:35). How presumptuous! It sounds arrogant, or maybe driven. They pulled no punches. What they wanted was the two most honorable places, the highest seats of prestige and glory. "Grant unto us that we may sit, one on thy right hand, and the other on thy left hand, in thy glory" (Mark 10:37). In the eastern court these positions were given to persons inferior only to the one on the throne.

The context of this request strips the mask off the nature of their ambition. Jesus had unburdened himself to his intimate friends. He had just told them about his impending suffering and death. The words were still fresh when James and John, insensitive to Jesus and his needs, asked for a personal favor.

Remember, ambition is not inherently wrong. Like any instinct of nature, it is capable of good or harm. Aspiring to be great is one thing; to be "the greatest," with no sensitivity to the suffering of others, is another. Either goal requires ambition. The problem with James and John was that their ambition was aimed at the wrong target. They were more concerned about gaining a crown of glory than helping Jesus face his crown of thorns. Coronation interested them, not crucifixion. They were preoccupied with thrones, not crosses. Pomp and power were desired, not providing fellowship for one who was about to suffer. And the clincher! Under the pressure of their drive to the top they failed to understand Jesus and his kingdom.

The Backward-Forward Principle

Mark gives us Jesus' answer. These two men asked for thrones and were offered instead a cup of sorrow and a baptism of suffering. Using two powerful metaphors, Jesus challenged the misdirected, misunderstood ambition of James and John. The cup symbolized the trials of life that are no respecter of persons. The baptism suggested being submerged in those experiences. Jesus asked James and John if they could bear what he was going to bear. He told them that without a cross there would be no crowns. If they wanted to be first, they must be willing to be last; to be served meant being a servant; to be supreme required being able to be submissive. The principle of discipleship is a backward-forward principle.

Greatness is obtained by pursuing opposite actions from what is usually practiced in the unbelieving world. Self-giving is the ingredient of greatness. You achieve not by expecting others to serve you, but by giving yourself in service to others. That is not the common attitude you see displayed in the modern marketplace. People are more accustomed to directing their ambition toward getting themselves there first.

Do you remember the Cabbage Patch dolls? People were frantic in their attempts to purchase them. Talk about eagerness; people stood hours in line just to acquire one. Some stole them, while a few even flew to London to purchase a doll. You also notice this feverish use of ambition at yard or garage sales. I remember the first time Janet and I scheduled one for 9:00 A.M. We were eating breakfast at eight when the first car arrived. Before nine we had sold the majority of what we sold all day. The next time we asked the early people to come back at nine. Some sat in their car and waited a half hour.

Most of us are well acquainted with the desire to get rather than to give, to be served instead of serving. You and I have probably scrambled with the best of them to be first in line. In one simple but profound statement, Jesus turns all this around and the "backward becomes forward." "Whosoever of you will be the chiefest, shall be servant of all" (Mark 10:44). That is what the backward-forward principle means. The remedy for the drivenness of misdirected ambition is to serve rather than be served. Are you like these two dis-

ciples? Are you speeding through life looking for your
Camelot?

Living Life in the Passing Lane

The first time I heard the phrase "living life in the passing
lane" was during my graduate program. Each day I traveled
Interstate 80 between Tipton and Iowa City, Iowa. This was
before the 55 mph speed limit. One fleet of trucks in particular traveled most of the time in the passing lane. They
were owned by the largest beef producers in the United
States. I saw at least four to six of these trucks each week
hauling meat to the East Coast. Commuters named the passing lanes in their honor. When we saw one in our rearview
mirror we stayed to the right. There are many ambitious
people like those truckers. At times I am like one of them.
Maybe you are too.

When you find yourself in the passing lane you are really
accelerating, seldom in cruise, and rarely going for a "joy
ride." You are on the go! Fathers work two jobs, saying, "It's
for the sake of my children." Many lose their children while
traveling in the passing lane. "A prize awaits the swift," they
say, "money, fame, and power, and the prize is only for the
swift."

Are you finding it hard to get out of the passing lane? Does
it seem like you're in a high-speed race? You are held by the
draft. Part of you wants out, but another part keeps saying,
"Now I'm really going fast." The problem is self-perpetuat-
ing. When caught in the passing lane, you end up going faster
than necessary. Your perceptions get disturbed. You are like
a lifetime gambler winning big at times but always raising the
stakes. The stakes are a life filled with stress; the results, a
breakdown in health.

Two types of persons get caught in the passing lane. They
are generally known as workaholics. One type I label *achiev-*
ers, the other, *drivers*. The first type is known as the ambi-

tion-ridden, the second has more recently been described as the Type A personality.

The Achievers: Ambition-ridden Persons

To be an achiever doesn't mean that you are necessarily an ambition-ridden person. But to be ambition-ridden usually means you are an achiever. There are also two kinds of achievers: the *arrivers* and the *activists*. If you are an arriver, you can celebrate your accomplishments. You enjoy the outcome of achieving. Arrivers are not trapped in the passing lane. You know how to use it when needed and when to move back into the flow of traffic. You even take time to read the historical markers or to enjoy pauses of inspiration at the scenic overlooks. When you are this kind of achiever you are not compulsive about your need to achieve. Arrivers don't live with a lingering feeling that they can't make it. Each time they accomplish something they enjoy it and can share it with others. I would like to be more like the achiever who is an arriver, wouldn't you?

Maybe you are more like an activist. You find it difficult to be satisfied with accomplishments. You get intensely involved, for example, in building your own home, and, when finished, you are unable to enjoy it. You constantly need more. Activists drive most of their trips in the passing lane. They keep close tabs on how many miles they travel each hour, seldom stopping to read anything, and passing the scenic overlooks with a fleeting feeling of regret that they don't have time to stop.

Have you noticed how skilled our society is in developing the activist type? Wayne Oates describes these persons as "workaholics." Harry Stack Sullivan uses the phrase the "ambition-ridden" and says there is "no dearth of these folk among us" *(Conceptions of Modern Psychiatry)*. They are persons who use others to advance their interests. Competition for them tends to be all-consuming. Manipulation for some is a refined skill. Either way, they are driving toward upward mobility.

The ambition-ridden person often ends up like a car I owned. My family affectionately called it the "Green Machine." We all felt sad when I finally sold it after 170,000 miles. It took us down many roads of fond memories. Once, however, I had to repair its transmission. It wouldn't shift correctly. Beginning in high gear, it stayed in high gear.

That is a picture of many activists. They are the ones who at their retirement dinners get complimented for thirty-five years without a vacation. As Wayne Oates observes in his delightful book *Workaholics, Make Laziness Work for You* (p. 67), "Slavery is often mistaken for devotion to duty."

One difficulty of the overachievers is that they find it hard to relax. When they schedule time to vacation, something in them keeps them from vacationing. Some take along their briefcase full of work. Have you ever gone on a vacation without any work projects? Try it sometime, you'll like it!

Overachievers find their fulfillment linked to being part of the upward pull. Their joy is in the climb and not in the fruits of completing it. And like vehicles in the passing lane, they use a lot of energy. Driven by misdirected ambition, they become overstressed and often experience poor health.

The Drivers: Type A Persons

Maybe you fit the Type A personality. The research on this kind of achiever was done by two cardiologists, Meyer Friedman and Ray H. Rosenman. They published their studies on life-styles and personality types as they relate to heart disease in their book *Type A Behavior and Your Heart*. The result of living under constant stress is that you endanger your physical health. Friedman and Rosenman found that the coronary system often fails under continuous stress. Type A persons are driven by a high need for achievement. They strive constantly to get ahead. Many are particularly vulnerable to the seduction of upward mobility.

If you are a Type A person, you tend to approach every waking moment as if it is the ninth inning of the seventh game of the World Series. When you drive in the passing lane your hand is near the horn. If anyone is in front, traveling at a slower pace, you will let them know that you are coming. Until recently Type A persons were mostly men, but women are now showing up in doctors' offices with many of the same signs. Type A behavior is becoming more common among women as they enter the once predominantly male work force in greater numbers.

Friedman and Rosenman found that Type A persons are often promoted in business, rewarded socially, and admired as dedicated and consecrated workers. They are usually competitive and rarely able to rest. They struggle with a basic need for self-worth. Though they often achieve their aspirations, they are seldom satisfied and never feel they can achieve all they want.

Type A persons, like activists, can also ruin a vacation. They only give a passing thought to relaxation and put off leisure activities. David is like that. He avoids leisure and resists taking vacations. As a small-business owner he rationalizes working because only he can do the job. The truth is, he hasn't trained anyone because he doesn't trust others to carry on while he is gone. When he does leave with his family, he worries and wonders what is going on at the office and has in the past returned early. The result is he only takes off when he feels he's about to "go under," in response to an emotional emergency, which is now more frequent. The research on persons like David show two aspects associated with eventual heart stress—competitive drive and impatience. Even when they succeed (and many do) they pay the enormous price of threatened health.

We Are Driven

There's another angle to this quest for success. Many of you have been urged to be the best, the strongest, and the most powerful. The "We're number one!" attitude is instilled in many of us from childhood. On a national scale this attitude is evident on all levels: transportation, athletics, technology, and military power. The drive for achievement is an all-pervasive attitude in too many of us.

In conversations with different people I learned that many believe that to be ambitious means to be driven. Have you noticed the way that attitude gets reinforced? An ad in *Fortune* magazine reads, "If you drive yourself today, you won't have to drive tomorrow." A Datsun commercial captures it best for me. Datsun uses the slogan, "We are driven!"

Ambition propelled by drivenness results in perfectionism. If you are a perfectionist, you probably already know it. Perfectionism is defined as the striving for the highest or the most perfect degree of a quality, trait, or accomplishment. You demand a lot of yourself. You strive to have things "just right"—the right color with the right color, everything in your office or home in its place, arriving and starting on time. These are commendable behaviors, until carried to extremes.

Psychiatrist Hugh Missildine finds most perfectionists to be obsessive and compulsive. His insightful book *Your Inner Child of the Past* describes them as driven. Their self-imposed demands exceed what is possible for themselves or for anyone. They are equally harsh on others. Life is viewed as a competition, a race to be won. To feel intimate and to give time to friendships is not easy for a person running at full speed. As Missildine says, "Any 'stopping' of his strivings in order to enjoy companionship or affection makes him fearful that he will lose the race" (p. 90).

In any field of endeavor, excellence is worthy of one's efforts. The distinction, however, between those who seek excellence and those who are perfectionists is that those in the first group find satisfaction in the results. They are happy with their achievements. Those in the second group are not free to enjoy what they accomplish. Instead, they experience feelings of inferiority and thoughts of "I'm not good enough, I must do better."

What drives you or me to reach the unreachable? I want to discuss two causes that promote perfectionism. One produces what I call the *perfecters,* the other I label the *strivers.* The perfecters are driven by their need to attain their idealized image or self, while the strivers are driven by feelings of inferiority. Both causes result in ambition being misdirected.

The Perfecters: The Idealized Self

If you are a perfecter, you often feel that you haven't arrived. Henry Adams apparently felt that way. Joseph Epstein describes him as one whose "genius was at war with his ambition" (*Ambition,* p. 31). Adams' genius was his capacity for reflection, scholarship, and political insight. His ambition was to leave his mark upon the world. That's the catch for Adams. Who would say that Adams did not leave his mark on the world? Adams would. He lived out his life never able to accept that he had achieved what he felt was worthwhile.

Maybe, like Adams, you struggle with what Karen Horney labels "the idealized self." You create an image that can never be attained. She describes it as the "tyranny of the should." The portrait of your idealized self is unrealistic. Horney calls it a form of self-inflation and a search for glory. When you feel compelled to become your idealized self you are experiencing an aspect of perfectionism. What counts is external success. You often disregard the inner content of what you are doing. Perfectionism is like racing dogs chasing the mechanical rabbits. They run night after night but never catch the rabbit. The perfecters among us are often in the pursuit of power or prestige. In *Neurosis and Human Growth,* Horney writes (p. 26), "The inner distress, to remedy which they started out on the chase for the phantom of glory, is still as great as ever."

The Strivers: The Inferiority Self

Feeling inferior spawns perfectionist behaviors. Most of us do feel some inferiority, so it is understandable that occasionally we become strivers. When you are a striver, your goal is to succeed and to gain superiority. To be the best, to sell the most, to run the fastest, to get there first are all part of striving. You will find strivers in all walks of life.

Horatio Alger success stories still happen in the 1980s. Many of those who make it to the top are often driven by feelings of inferiority. One Silicon Valley electronics millionaire, Porter Hurt, grew up in a family that couldn't afford to buy a house. Hurt is raising his family in a three-million-dollar mansion where all the furniture is custom-made. One of his prime motivating factors was his vivid memory of back-breaking work and hard times during his earlier years. ("Success, The Chase Is Back in Style Again," *U.S. News & World Report,* Oct. 3, 1983, p. 63.)

Alfred Adler believes that everyone wrestles with feelings of inferiority. He contends that if you did not feel inferior, you would not have any desire to go beyond the immediate. Adler writes, "We strive because we feel inferior, and we overcome our feeling of inferiority by successful striving" (*The Education of Children,* p. 77; Greenberg Publisher, 1930). Your feelings of inferiority are not necessarily abnormal. In fact, Adler believes they are a motivator for improvement.

However, your inferior self can accumulate some strong feelings that threaten your self-image. These feelings are often rooted in your childhood. If you were hindered in experiencing success as a child, you may now be compensating by striving harder to achieve. Or maybe you acquired negative attitudes about yourself. I listen to many capable persons who frequently put themselves down. A young man shared with me that he never felt accepted by his family. He continues to strive for acceptance by being the best worker, the best student, the best "whatever." What a relief it was for him when he began to realize that he didn't need to be the best of anything to experience God's acceptance. The person who strives the most is usually not able to enjoy his or her achievements. High achievers often have a great need for appreciation.

Prescriptions for Reducing Your Speed

Are you hard put to find space in your daily schedule for a change of pace? Do you rush from one obligation to the next at a breathless rate of speed? If you tend to be ambition-ridden or a Type A personality and are driven by your idealized self or by feelings of inferiority, you probably are in need of prescriptions for reducing your speed—prescriptions, because home remedies are not strong enough to reroute the ambitious energies that propel you along in the passing lane.

The following prescriptions are designed to moderate your speed. They are not meant to be roadblocks for your ambition, but course corrections for its misdirected use. If they help you to enjoy your ambition, that will be great! If they reduce your perfectionist tendency to a level that produces productive living, that will be even better! You deserve more from your ambition than achievements that don't satisfy and schedules that are frantic.

Practice Your Right to Relax

In a delightful tongue-in-cheek manner Wayne Oates has written *Workaholics, Make Laziness Work for You,* a book addressed "to the driven ones, the work-addicted ones, the people who have *earned* the right to be lazy." Oates affirms the ambitious, conscientious hard workers. They are often the "burden bearers" of their communities. But he is also quick to "read them their rights" to claim freedom from work addiction and the "tyranny of an ambition-ridden conscience." You may be one of those who have earned your right to relax. Yet something keeps you from laying claim to this right. That's why you need this prescription. Practice it! You've earned it!

Some of you may feel I am asking you to give up your ambition. Not true. Relaxation is necessary for any ambitious person who wants to live productively. You need it! All work and no play not only makes Johnny a dull boy, it's not God's design for healthy living. God's work–rest ratio is 6 to 1. This is the principle of the sabbath: six days of labor, one day of rest (Ex. 23:12). Rest is linked to relaxation and worship. Relaxation, like worship, needs practice. Here are some specific remedies.

1. *Reexamine your calendar.* Do you find time set aside for recreation? Schedule relaxation into your calendar. You are worth it! Block off time marked "me." Then you can honestly tell someone, "That evening is taken." Most of us need a certain amount of "me time" in order to provide "other time." Make your calendar work for you. Don't be its slave. If you are not in charge of your time, you will be ruled by the requests of others.

2. *Make your relaxation restful.* The irony of the ambition-ridden is that they work at relaxing. Trying to relax can be as exhausting as your hectic work load. Plan to return from your vacation a few days early. Relaxing at home a day before returning to your job is icing on the cake. Choose hobbies that do not need to be financially profitable or rob you of sleep or add tension to your life. Hobbies are meant to be diversions and activities that renew.

3. *Let the process work.* Remember, any treatment takes time to take effect. To rush relaxation is a contradiction. You need time for what in good Quaker tradition is called "cen-

tering down." This process begins by clearing the mind of business before the periods of quiet reflection and meditation are experienced. Your relaxation will also need some time to make the transition from work to rest. Remember, this antidote requires practice.

Build Pace Into Your Race

If you tend to be a Type A person, you race the clock. More done in less time is your goal. Like other hard-driving individuals, you have little pace in your race. This prescription is like the previous one. Both are given to build rhythm into your living. Everyone needs a change of pace, a balance between work and play, strain and rest, fatigue and refreshment, noise and silence. Here are some ways to make this prescription take hold.

1. *Plan for pace.* Pace-planning can be applied to many aspects of your day and life. One way is to be ready to leave fifteen minutes early in the morning. You may shock your spouse, but you will enjoy fifteen anxious-free minutes to use any way you want.

2. *Vary your speed.* Find ways each day to alter the rate at which you are going. Give yourself moments when you are not producing at maximum efficiency. Instead of taking the bus to your corner, get off a few stops early and walk the rest of the way. Walking is a nice time to file your thoughts before arriving home. Einstein believed that when you take different routes home you will expand the use of your brain. Look for other ways to interrupt your routine. Variety is the spice of life.

3. *Change your work pace.* Your life is full of activities and actions. What you may need are some breaks in the action. When you push yourself with constant work you often experience negative payoff. Fatigue, anxious nights, and more errors are just a few signs of overwork. Use breaks to interrupt your intensity. Turn to easier tasks when you need to back off from a more difficult one for a short change of pace.

4. *Enjoy moments of silence.* If you work in a factory or in a large city, you probably find it hard to retreat from the noise of your surroundings. Creativity will be needed to gain a few moments of periodic silence. One of my first jobs after high school was with Chrysler Corporation. I worked the grave-yard shift in the paint and trim department. Frequently during lunch I would sit in an unfinished car body to eat and rest. Once I fell asleep and was awakened by the foreman. Fortunately for me, he understood the problems of an eigh-teen-year-old Wisconsin farm boy trying to cope with the noise and tensions of that Los Angeles industrial setting.

Treat Yourself Well

You may be surprised with this prescription. I received it from a friend who invited me to a basketball game. We hadn't seen each other for a while so we spent much of the time bringing each other up-to-date about our work and in-terests. I can't tell you the score of the game, but I will never forget his parting words: "Treat yourself well this week!" Those can be life-freeing words to a perfectionist whose am-bition gets misdirected.

I am not suggesting that you are to be selfish or self-cen-tered. I am asking you to give yourself the respect and kind-ness that is due you. Perfectionists are often more critical and demanding of themselves than anyone else, including God. Do you know, you are not inferior in God's view? Neither are you perfect! That's just it. You are loved so much by God that he sent his Son to die for you. Each one of you is that important to God. As E. Stanley Jones, the great missionary to India, wrote, "If He died for me, there must be some-thing in me worth dying for. So surrender to Christ. . . . You are not a worm, nor a wonder. You are the ordinary becom-ing the extraordinary, all due to Him. So you can be your-self because you are His self. You are free to be" (*Victory Through Surrender*, pp. 45–46; Abingdon Press, 1966). So do yourself a favor. Make a note of ways you can be kind to yourself. Like taking a daily vitamin, do something nice for yourself each day. You usually treat others as you treat yourself.

Has living turned for you into a search for your Camelot? Do you feel caught in a passing lane of unfulfilling achievements? Place your time, timing, and times into the context of God's eternity. If you do, you will be more able to separate things that matter from those that are trivial. The ambition-ridden person lacks perspective and is unable to see what is trivial and what is important. The days of our years are threescore and ten, or eighty if we are strong, says Psalm 90:10. Learn how short your life is, and you will become wise. Such a perspective lowers your strain and stress, raises your sense of humor, and eases your life back into a health-giving pace. Take time, therefore, to fix your attention on this eternal God, and the temporary demands of life will undergo a transforming grace and you will exert your energies according to a larger design of God than your own.

Part III

AMBITION AS FRIEND

Chapter 5

Choosing Your Positions: Ambition Inner-directed

> He it is, who coming after me is preferred before me, whose shoe-latchet I am not worthy to unloose.
>
> *John 1:27*

The character of your ambition is within you. What you personally express as ambition first begins as part of your inner life before it becomes public to others. Thus, the content of your outer behavior is a reflection of the context of your inner life.

The Model of an Inner-directed Ambition

Ambition is honorable when it comes from an inner life that is honorable. For as we have seen, ambition by itself is neither moral nor immoral, neither friend nor enemy. Primarily, it is a common energy or drive inherent in the nature of each person. However, ambition does not remain unconnected, nor is it expressed in isolation. You will note that your ambition is linked to desires, goals, hopes, and aspirations. The quality of its meaning is directly related to the excellence of its inner source within you. The goodness of your desires are as ethical as your motives.

Jesus and the Inner Life

The importance of your inner life was clearly taught by Jesus. He stated that the character of your inner attitudes shapes the quality of your outer actions. He told a crowd once, "There is nothing from without a man, that entering into him can defile him: but the things which come out of him, those are they that defile the man" (Mark 7:15). On another occasion he taught his disciples, "A good man out of the good treasure of his heart bringeth forth that which is good; and an evil man out of the evil treasure of his heart bringeth forth that which is evil" (Luke 6:45).

Jesus did not imply that you are to be afraid to be ambitious. Neither are you to discourage ambition as a protection against its misuse. You do not need to avoid ambition because of its potential excesses. You can be ambitious for the good of others, and for the betterment of one's life. When you choose a godly ambition, you give a Christian character to your accomplishments. Yet you can degrade ambition by using it for selfish and vain purposes.

An Inner Life Expressed

The English poet Philip Sidney wrote, "To be ambitious of true honor and of real glory and perfection of our nature is the very principle and incentive of virtue; but to be ambitious of titles, place, ceremonial request, and civil pageantry, is as vain and little as the things are that we count" (Carroll E. Simox, comp., *A Treasury of Quotations on Christian Themes,* p. 67; Seabury Press, 1975). What's the difference? What enables you to keep ambition in its proper proportion and perspective? What makes ambition your friend rather than your enemy?

I believe the answer is found within you. The outworking of your ambition and the positions you seek are extensions of your internal spiritual life. When you develop your spiritual life you will build a base within that will enable you to serve others. The quality of your love for God and neighbor, as Jesus declared, is expressed in the quality of your love for your own self as a child of God. As a person directed from within, guided by the Spirit of God, you are free to choose your genuine calling and place in life.

John the Baptist was an inner-directed person. He was committed to know the inner direction of God's Spirit. In Chapter 1, I discussed the dilemma John felt about Jesus. He had some honest questions to answer. He wanted to clarify his role in reference to Jesus. John felt clear about his calling. He gladly embraced it. He knew himself. He knew his place in the unfolding plan of God. The certainty of his call and position became an anchor when the pressures came. The sterling quality of his inner ambitions kept him from wavering. He knew he was not to receive titles but to give them. His popularity was not to increase but to decrease. Those who had become his followers were to leave him in order to follow Jesus. Now that's a humbling position to be in. I'm not sure how gracious I would be. Are you?

An Inner Life Tested

The test of John's inner desires came without fail. Community dignitaries asked John to identify himself. They even suggested some titles he might claim. Here was a chance to capitalize on his unique popularity. He might even allow his inquirers to assume some things by remaining unclear about his image. John did none of these things. He set the record straight, clearly and specifically. "I'm not any of those whom you suggest that I might be. I am a voice, a mouthpiece of God's word to you. My role is to alert you to the coming of One mightier than any of us. This One is preferred before me. I am not even worthy to untie the straps of his sandals." That's what John told the authorities. What a model of inner integrity and moral ambition! Any greatness John received came from the greatness of the One he proclaimed.

John wasn't less ambitious because of his choice. The principle to him was clear: "Whosoever exalteth himself shall be abased; and he that humbleth himself shall be exalted" (Luke 14:11). He modeled what Jesus meant: "But when thou art bidden, go and sit down in the lowest room; that when he that bade thee cometh, he may say unto thee, Friend, go up higher" (Luke 14:10). His ambition was in harmony with his inner life. He had no struggle with pointing his followers to Jesus, as the "one sent from God." John was an inner-directed person who expressed an honorable ambition.

The Meaning of an Inner-directed Ambition

Ambition, like any fuel or energy, needs direction and control. The primary source for both its direction and its control is the presence of God within you. Inner-directed ambition is different from self-directed ambition. Ambition directed inward produces self-awareness. Self-directed ambition produces self-centeredness. The results of self-awareness are insight and self-growth. Insight about your needs and potentials enables you to live life with spiritually discerned moral values and priorities.

Ambition becomes a friend, then, when it produces growth in your self-knowledge and in your inner spiritual maturity. This growth helps you to know your strengths and your weaknesses, your potentials and your limitations. The truth about your life enables you to tap into the capacities created within you. Self-truth leads your inner prayers to discover the One who is "the Truth, Christ in you." To become inner-directed is to experience the presence of God within you and to live not merely for yourself but for others under the rule of Christ's indwelling presence. Dietrich Bonhoeffer, the pastor-theologian who died in a concentration camp during World War II, wrote that a "man for others" is the one who is also "in tune with himself." You cannot be in tune with yourself without being in touch with the One who created you.

Inner-Ambition Illustrated

The movie *Chariots of Fire* presents a contrast in its two major characters between inner-directed and self-directed ambition. Eric Liddell and Harold Abrahams both seek to win gold medals at the 1924 Olympics. Liddell reflects inner-directed ambition, Abrahams represents self-directed ambition. The difference is evident.

Eric Liddell runs out of a natural love for running. He senses within him a power, a God-given talent that he appreciates as a gift. Running for him is an extension of his inner faith in God. This is vividly portrayed in two different scenes.

The first scene follows a victory. He is addressing an admiring crowd. With the rain falling on his face he tells them, "The power comes from within. Jesus told us, 'Behold, the Kingdom of God is within you. If with all your hearts, you truly seek me, you shall ever surely find me.' If you commit yourself to the love of Christ, then that is how you run the straight race." (W. J. Weatherby et al., *Chariots of Fire*, p. 53, Screenplay by Colin Welland; Quicksilver Books, 1981; used by permission.) The second scene comes after his sister expresses her disappointment with Eric's commitment to running. She feels his ambition "to run faster than any man" takes too much time from the mission church they serve. But more than that, she is afraid his missionary call to China is being replaced by this consuming ambition to run. In a very personal and powerful scene, Eric asks his sister, Jenny, to take a walk. During the walk he explains to her that his passion for running is not disconnected from his commitment to ministry. "Jenny, Jenny, you've got to understand. I believe that God made me for a purpose. For China. But He also made me fast, and when I run I feel His pleasure." To run, for Eric Liddell, is to honor God, who, he believes, has given him the ability and the inner ambition to run fast.

The test of Eric's inner values comes; it always does. He

makes the Olympic team. He is favored to win a medal. Then he learns that the final heat of his only event is scheduled on Sunday morning. This is in conflict with his commitment to worship. He makes his concern known to the team officials. They try to persuade him to reconsider. But out of commitment to his inner values and priorities he withdraws from his best event.

Self-Ambition Illustrated

Harold Abrahams also has a passion to run, but his passion is driven by a self-directed ambition. He wants to run in order to beat all challengers, to prove his worth. There's the difference. He is motivated by a defensive struggle to protect his self-image. He is not really free to choose to run. It is a compulsion, a drivenness, like a life-and-death struggle to be superior. He needs to win.

This self-directed ambition is also illustrated in two different scenes. Early in the film Harold shares with a new friend the deep pent-up resentment that smolders within him because of prejudice he feels toward him as a Jew. With a hurt determination, he says, "It's an ache, a helplessness, an anger. . . . They treat me like some rare species of ape. . . . I'm going to take them on. One by one. All of them. And run them off their feet."

The second scene comes after his first loss, in a race won by Eric Liddell. Alone in the stands, an hour after the race, he sits beaten. When found by the young lady he later marries, who tries to console him, he says impatiently, "I don't run to take beatings. I run to win. If I can't win, I won't run." She confronts him with his childlike behavior and he replies, "It's not the losing, Syb. It's me. After all that work, I lost, and now God knows what do I aim for?" (*Chariots of Fire,* p. 77.)

The drive to prove himself grows more intense. Abrahams secures a coach and defies the advice of his school's authorities who question his methods but secretly share his compulsion for their own selfish reasons. He trains long and hard. There is no relaxed pleasure in running for him. He runs with one obsession, to beat the one who is faster—Eric Liddell. His goal is self-directed and his ambition to achieve almost consumes him.

Do these two "chariots of fire" win their gold medals? A teammate withdraws from a later race to let Liddell run in his place. No longer in his best event, but with a belief in his God-given ability to run, Eric draws from an inner capacity and wins his gold medal. His sister is there to celebrate his victory. Eric does go to China as a missionary. (He died in a Japanese prison camp close to the end of World War II.)

Abrahams runs in that Sunday event where he hoped to meet Liddell. He too wins and receives a gold medal, but he has lost his chance for revenge. He does not attend his victory celebration. The drive to win is a self-directed compulsion to prove his self-worth. The direction of his ambition has in the end consumed his capacity to celebrate. The contrast between Eric Liddell and Harold Abrahams is a classic illustration of the difference between an inner-directed and a self-directed ambition.

The Source of an Inner-directed Life

To describe yourself as an inner-directed person who is not interested in your self is not accurate. You do not direct your ambition inward to depreciate yourself. Self-worth is needed by all of us. You rightfully desire to feel worthy and loved. Jesus pointed this out in the second great commandment (Mark 12:29–31). Psychologist William Glasser echoes what Jesus taught when he suggests that one basic need of human nature is to feel worthwhile to yourself and to others. Genuine self-worth does not become false pride.

Self-worth is an inner quality. You mature your self-worth by giving attention to your inner life. Hugh Missildine says it clearly: "You can't turn against yourself and have inner security" (p. 19). Chapter 3 described ambition when directed

toward selfishness, "What's in it for me?" Inner-directed ambition is concerned for your moral character, not for what
you can get. You attend to your inner life in order to develop the quality of your "beingness." The freedom to
choose lesser seats of honor is the expression of an inner being that doesn't always need the external trappings of seating
arrangements in order to feel fulfilled. What is the source
that enables you to grow an inner-directed life? What keeps
ambition directed inward from becoming self-promoting?
The answer, I believe, is found in your understanding of
love.

The theme that runs throughout the Bible is, "You are
loved!" In spite of our unworthiness, "God so loved . . . that
he gave his only begotten son, that whosoever believeth in
him should not perish, but have everlasting life" (John 3:16).
This assurance of love can capture your inner being and lead
you to yield your ambitions to God. Because "God so loved"
you, you can learn to love what he loves. He loves you! I'm
not suggesting that you stand before a mirror and say, "Mirror, mirror, on the wall, who's the fairest one of all?" The
meaning of an inner-directed self is found in those who know
God's love and accept that they are loved. I'm talking about
persons who love themselves with a realization that they are
free to give only that which they possess. Your service to
others is the natural expression of an inner life that knows
the love of God.

The Marks of an Inner-directed Ambition

The most meaningful way to direct your ambitious energies is with the spiritual guidance of a deep love for God. I
do not mean, of course, that it's necessary to believe in God
to be ambitious or to achieve security and success. These are
often associated with worldly achievements. But I do believe that spiritual peace and power at the center of your life
is necessary if you hope to enjoy your ambition to its fullest.

For only when you discover some ultimate purpose in all you achieve will your ambitions be transformed into truly meaningful expressions.

What then are some marks of an inner-directed life? Here are three I want to highlight. You see them reflected in the life of John the Baptist. Each mark is like a badge forged in the experience of life and expressed out of John's commitment to his calling and to Jesus Christ as God's Son.

Faith for Taking Leaps

The life of John the Baptist was marked by faith. He believed in what was not yet seen. There was leap-taking in his preaching. He predicted that there was One coming mightier than he. So strong was his faith in the future coming of Jesus that he wanted others to be prepared for that event.

Faith will shape your inner ambitions. First, belief in God and belief in yourself nurture your life. Then from this inner life comes faith in the possibility of the future. When confidence in the future is waning or when people become only present-centered, they seem to lose ambition. As Epstein wondered, "Whether the loss of belief in ambition has caused this loss of confidence in the future, or the loss of confidence in the future has caused the loss of belief in ambition, is difficult to say. But that the two are connected is not arguable" (*Ambition*, p. 5).

Faith doesn't mean you will not feel some anguish in the face of an uncertain future. Most of us experience anxiety prior to some important decision. Many young couples feel twinges of doubt the evening before their wedding day. I like the quote that says, "It's not important that you have butterflies in your stomach. What is important is that you teach them to fly in formation." That's what faith will do for your ambition. Faith means founding your life upon a foundation that is eternal, upon Christ. Faith holds you captive to Christ so that your own self is free to take leaps.

Would you like to be "marked" by faith? Samuel Shoe-

maker believed that you develop faith through spiritual ex-
periments. You learn faith by being near those who are faithful. Look around you. The evidence of faith is there. You
will see persons who believe without reservation that God is,
that he is love, and that he has power to help you through
troubled waters. There are those who meet sorrow and pain
with serenity, who respond to shortcomings in others with
patience, and who meet needs with a helping hand. Be a participant in faith, not just a spectator! You must open yourself to the stream of God's power. And Shoemaker advised,
"Act as if the whole thing, the reality and love of God as re-
vealed by Christ . . . were all true. Never mind if you have
doubts. . . . Behave as if you believed!" (Arthur Gordon, *A
Touch of Wonder,* pp. 100–104). The value of faith is using
it. Exercise faith and you will verify faith!

Hope for Making Dreams

You also see hope in John the Baptist. When Jesus came
to him to be baptized, it was their first meeting. John's first
words were full of hope: "Behold the Lamb of God, which
taketh away the sin of the world!" (John 1:29). When you exercise hope you will experience the creative presence of
Christ in your life.

Hope is like hearing a bird singing in the darkness in anticipation of the dawn. Hope is trust, not despair; humility,
not arrogance. Hope is confidence that when all the options
seem disastrous, the last word has not been spoken.

Your ambition finds meaning in hope. Hope keeps you
free of resignation. Hope believes that the impossible is possible. Your crooked paths are straighter; your obstacles more
like stepping-stones in the presence of hope. When your ambitions are marked by hope, situations that formerly were trials to be endured become opportunities to be celebrated. It
is true! Things turn out best for those who make the best of
the way things turn out.

Your ambition may seem stifled, but in the context of

hope it is not silenced. Norman Cousins believes that the capacity for hope is the greatest fact of life. Hope is the launching pad for plans. Hope, he believes, shapes your destiny and provides you a sense of direction ("The Case for Hope," *Saturday Review,* Dec. 26, 1970, p. 18). Ambitions are energized by hope.

Hope creates dreams. If you are an inner-directed person, you live life with a sense of hope. Hope and ambition make dreams become possibilities. When your dreams are strong and clear, no realities can stand against them. What do you dream about? Those dreams are within you. This is another reason for knowing yourself. To discover who you are is to uncover your potential for making dreams. That's what hope does.

You see this link between hope and ambition in the life of Eric Lund. He was twenty-two when he lost his struggle with leukemia. At seventeen Eric learned of his illness. His ambitions remained full of hope. He went to college, joined the soccer team, and experienced the ups and downs of his illness. Yet his hope never waned. It was still evident near the end of his earthly life. His mother described one of her final visits with her son in "Walk in the World for Me," in the July 1973 *Reader's Digest* (used by permission). Eric had been summing up his life, feeling again the good memories while there still was time. He was telling his mother without telling her: Be ready, be strong. Then quietly, toward evening, he said to her, "Do something for me. Leave a little early. Walk a few blocks and look at the sky. Walk in the world for me." Ambition cloaked in hope will always find a way to live on!

Patience for Accepting Situations

Did you notice the patience of John the Baptist? You see it manifested in his life when the religious authorities wanted to make him more than who he was (John 1:19ff.). Later, in prison, his capacity for long-suffering was again evident. But

the unexpected test of his patience came when Jesus re-
quested John to baptize him. John couldn't understand that
request. He wasn't able to comprehend what it meant, but
he obeyed. In each of these incidents John patiently accepted his situation. He was able to wait for events to un-
fold and for his understanding to become informed. His capacity to endure is another mark of an inner-directed life.

Patience, then, is your ability to hold back your ambition
for a more honorable and long-term purpose. When you are
patient you do not demand that your desires be met immediately. Tolerant people are not prisoners to immature urges.
They are free to choose when to release their ambition and
where to channel it. When you are able to be long-suffering
you enjoy a sense of control. Your creativity is not ex-
hausted in compulsive living. Patience is a virtue of your inner maturity.

On the other hand, impatience is common to most of us.
Maybe you feel like those who want their future now. You
live in a culture where a quick fix is the norm. We have fast
food, fast checkouts, fast lanes, and instant anything. Super-
sonic speed and computers are bringing rapid change into
your life. You can almost have tomorrow yesterday. Consequently, you may not be in the habit of waiting. Patience is
not nurtured. Instead, when delay is encountered, impatience is experienced.

I believe that you develop forbearance by squarely con-
fronting the unpleasant side of your life. You must accept the
fact of your situations. I believe that the only valid basis for
productive living is to assume that unpleasant things do happen; they can happen to any of us. When you take the attitude that things aren't always going to be perfect, you will
soften disappointments when events don't go as you had
hoped.

Patience has never been one of my virtues. I don't enjoy
window-shopping unless I am looking for something specific. Then I usually work at it vigorously until I have pur-

chased it. Getting behind a slow line of cars still generates frustration. I like airplane trips that start and end on time. There is no question about it. I am one of those who need more patience. If you are like me, there is one thing I have discovered. There is no easy formula for acquiring patience; only a subtle blend of wisdom and self-control can increase it. You must learn that premature action can often spoil everything. You just have to believe, with Emerson, that "if the single man plant himself indomitably on his instincts, and there abide, the huge world will come round to him." The truth is, "If you can't change the facts, try bending your attitudes to fit them!"

The "Making" of an Inner-directed Ambition

An inner-directed life is a spiritual journey, not a destination. If your goal to develop your spiritual life becomes the end in itself, that end can lead to self-righteousness. Also, your goals for making ambition an inner quality should not be the final aim, but more like stepping-stones or way stations on your journey through life.

Neither is your inner life unrelated to the rest of your existence, like some walled-off area surrounded with NO TRESPASSING signs. The writer of Proverbs 4:23 contends that out of your inner life come the issues of life. Jesus affirms that your inner being is the source of life. He said that the kingdom of God is within us (Luke 17:21). He taught that from within comes evil or good, pride or humility (Luke 6:45). You and I are to give careful attention to the content of our inner life. To help us we need to develop disciplined acts and dedicated attitudes.

Develop Disciplined Acts

The key to spiritual growth is discipline Actually, the words "discipline" and "disciple" are derived from the same root. A disciple then is one who is mastered by the Spirit of

God. Without discipline your life is more like a ship without a helmsman. You are tossed "to and fro" with no direction for sail or self. Discipline leads to discovery, discovery leads to deliverance, and deliverance leads to doxology. Discipline assumes you can change. Through discipline you bring quality and spirituality into your living. Here are a few suggestions related to discipline.

1. *Choose acts of discipline that build spiritual quality.* Richard Foster categorizes spiritual disciplines as inward, outward, or corporate in focus in his book *Celebration of Discipline.* Inward disciplines include meditation and prayer. Outward disciplines are represented by simplicity and service. The corporate list includes worship and celebration. You may want to choose at least one from each area. Plan to give your full commitment to acts that develop those spiritual dimensions. Spiritual development is basic to inner quality.

2. *Develop disciplines that are relevant to your own life.* Do not live in bondage to another's expectations. You are not to be a carbon copy of someone else. Young David wisely refused King Saul's armor. If your acts of discipline are to have any transforming effect, they must meet you at *your* cutting edge. I believe that God's presence is never more powerful than at the points of our needs.

3. *Practice discipline realistically.* Change doesn't usually happen overnight. Habits are formed slowly. Give time a chance to nurture your inner life. Also practice discipline, but do not keep score. You are not out to make records, but to break unwanted patterns and to develop new ones. Here are some guidelines. *Define* what you want to accomplish or to become. *Develop* disciplines that are suited for you and that will aid your progress toward what you have selected as your goal. *Dedicate* yourself to those disciplines. *Discover* a friend to whom you can be accountable for your goals. *Delight* in the freedom that fulfilled disciplines will bring to you.

Develop Dedicated Attitudes

"The greatest discovery of our generation," said William James, "is that human beings by changing their inner attitudes can change the outer aspects of their lives." Attitudes are the real springs of action. They form the character and quality of your inner life. Attitudes of kindness or resentment, criticism or praise, generosity or stinginess are only a reflection of the many attitudes you and I can possess. Dedicate yourself to understanding your attitudes. Devote yourself to building into your life those attitudes which develop inner quality of spirit and expression. The two attitudes that I believe are vital to the development of our inner being are the attitudes of seeking and submitting.

1. *Be a seeker after truth.* You can always learn something new. A local university initiated a program where persons over sixty-five years of age were eligible to enroll in classes for only a small fee. One seventy-three-year-old participant said, "I have never enjoyed learning anymore than right now." There is nothing more exciting than to learn a new truth, gain a new insight, acquire some new knowledge. No one can take away truth, insight, or knowledge.

There is another dimension of seeking after truth. When you dedicate yourself to know truth you will be led to the Truth—Jesus Christ. Jesus said, "I am the way, the truth, and the life" (John 14:6). And "the truth," he confirmed, "shall make you free" (John 8:32). So seek truth! Truth about your life and about God is vital to developing your inner life.

2. *Be submitted to accept truth.* "Walk in the light" is the biblical admonition. Truth becomes part of you only after you submit yourself to it. Actually, the attitudes of seeking and submitting are companions. To seek truth means to become submitted to know truth. To submit to truth is to believe in truth. When you discover the truth in Jesus Christ you are confronted with submission to that truth. And you only be-

come free when you submit to Christ as truth. Submission is an inner attitude. You can be very obedient in all your behaviors, but unless you are inwardly submitted to Christ you are not free. George Matheson wrote words to a hymn that captures this paradox: "Make me a captive, Lord, And then I shall be free; Force me to render up my sword, And I shall conqueror be."

When you submit to Christ as the Truth, you are free to forgive shortcomings, to release resentments, and to give up your own rights for the good of others. You become free to love your enemies and pray for those who persecute you. To seek the truth, to submit yourself to the truth, is the cornerstone of a life that is truly free. In submission to the higher authority of Christ's presence in you, your ambition becomes your friend.

Chapter 6

Maturing Your Service: Ambition Other-directed

For even the Son of man came not to be ministered unto, but to minister, and to give his life a ransom for many.

Mark 10:45

This verse from Mark's Gospel is clear. The sign of a higher ambition is serving others! Jesus not only taught this, he practiced it. During his final meal with his disciples he became their servant. Girding himself with a towel, he took a water basin and washed their feet. When he finished he commanded them to do likewise, saying, "For I have given you an example, that ye should do as I have done to you" (John 13:15).

The "Sign" of a Higher Ambition

The commitment to servanthood continues to be the response of Christian faith. As Christian disciples, you and I are called to perfect our service. Your ambition is never more worthy than when expressed in concern for the cares and needs of others.

Like many good intentions, however, being a servant is easier "said than done." Do you find that true for yourself? I do. Let's be fair. You know what it takes to keep your life afloat. Sometimes there is little energy left to give to others. How many of your neighbors do you know? That's one of those interesting barometers of our society. It was six weeks before I visited my newest neighbors. They only lived next door! I justified it by being under the pressure to write this chapter. Isn't that ironic? But as many of you know, that's a fact of life. Yet Jesus made it clear. The ultimate expression of our life is to be service.

A Servant Attitude

Earlier I invited you to do some reflecting about the meaning of ambition. How are you doing? Has your ambition felt more like an enemy than a friend? If so, you're not alone. Many of us struggle with how to handle our yearnings to achieve. In Chapter 5, I discussed the importance of developing the inner life. Now it's time to look at the outward direction of our drives. Our ambitions flow from our inner life—outward—toward the objects that are important to us.

Do you remember the mother of James and John asking Jesus to promote her two enterprising sons? That request got a poor press review among their colleagues. The other disciples were quite put out by her bold request. But put yourself in her shoes. Her motives may have been innocent. She was proud of her sons. They were among the Twelve, part of an up-and-coming ministry. Jesus was talking about building kingdoms. Here was a break for her boys, who had left their fishing nets. And remember, she didn't ask that her sons occupy the center throne; that belonged to Jesus.

The response Jesus gave became a teachable moment. Jesus was right up-front with what he wanted them to learn. He said, "Whosoever will be great among you, shall be your minister: And whosoever of you will be the chiefest, shall be servant of all" (Mark 10:43-44). What a contrast to their concept of vocation! Then, before those words could be debated in their minds, Jesus made his point. "For even the Son of man came not to be ministered unto, but to minister, and to give his life a ransom for many" (Mark 10:45). Jesus was crystal-clear. "Be a servant, give to others!" That's the attitude he wanted for them and still wants for us.

Resistance to Service

Does your mental image of a servant make you uncomfortable? After all, that occupation isn't listed among the top ten positions desired by college graduates. Have you known anyone whose vocational interest was to be a servant? Can you imagine someone's telling you, "I'm really zealous about being a servant. That's my passion"? Even the phrase "servant leadership" seems to contradict itself. Servants are persons who are in the background, usually not leaders. Yet if I understand what Jesus taught, that's what it means to follow him.

Maybe you have overlooked the call to mature your service. In today's looking-out-for-number-one society, the art of unselfish living isn't the most practiced discipline. You and I are surrounded by the attitude that "no one else is going to watch out for you unless you do." I admit feeling that way, especially when I get caught with some poorly made product that needs frequent repair. Furthermore, the service we see modeled isn't that perfect! Robert Greenleaf is right: "We are becoming a nation that is dominated by large institutions . . . and these big institutions are not serving us well" (*Servant Leadership,* p. 1; Paulist Press, 1977). Do you know what he means? If you have tried to find a clerk in a large discount store, you do. I waited fifteen minutes recently for a clerk. There were three calls for "customer assistance in the Hardware Department." I finally went to the manager. He called for someone by name. You guessed it. He didn't show up either, and I left. Resistance to service comes in many forms.

Maybe you resist service because you are afraid you will get too involved. Perhaps some of you are so entangled in your own personal pursuits that you have little time and energy left to offer help to another. President Kennedy's chal-

lenge, "Ask not what your country can do for you; ask what
you can do for your country," is inspiring but easily resisted.

Service from Strength

If you resist the servant attitude because it suggests weakness, you are in for a surprise. The apostle Paul recognized
the rightful place of the servant heart. He frequently described himself as "a servant of Jesus Christ" (Rom. 1:1).
However, he served out of strength. He wrote, "For I sup-
pose I was not a whit behind the very chiefest apostles" (II
Cor. 11:5).

Paul wasn't bragging. He was quick to admit that his
strength came from Christ's presence in his life. He knew
that "all things" could only be done because Christ "strength-
eneth me" (Phil. 4:13). The strength came from his servant
model—Jesus Christ. Your strength to serve also comes from
"Christ in you." He gave his life for you, so you can give
yourself in service to others. The service you give is not
given to justify your goodness, but to express your gratitude
to Christ, who gave his all for you. His strength in you
enables you to give hope to others.

Recently I read about a modern-day good Samaritan. A
Michigan woman and her family were seriously injured in an
auto accident near my home. During her six-week hospitali-
zation people in the area, strangers to her, acted as servants.
One family heard of her plight and lodged her relatives. Others loaned clothes, and many visited her in the hospital. Her
husband wrote: "Several times I didn't believe we were going to make it. There were so many nice people there that I
hate to mention the names because I would leave somebody
out" (*Lexington* (Ky.) *Herald-Leader,* Aug. 6, 1983; used by
permission).

Look for your servant opportunities. You'll find them.
And when you do, respond, reach out to them. As you em-
brace them, you will become an extension of Christ's servanthood in your world. There is no other higher ambition,

Christ said, than to do the will of the Father. For Christ, the "will of the Father" was to serve even "the least of these." We are to go and do likewise.

The "Servanthood" of Downward Mobility

There is a new phrase gaining in popularity: "downward mobility." It's the opposite of the upward mobility discussed in Chapter 4. Downward mobility is a reaction to our culture's all-consuming drive to climb the ladder of success. To move downward means stepping down from the positions occupied by one's parents.

Upward mobility, you remember, tries to sell you the bill of goods that the only way to go is up, that bigger is better. If you work hard and long, you can achieve the good life— even better than your parents. Sound familiar? But ladder-climbing hasn't always been appealing to some of our sons and daughters. Have your well-built ladders been ignored by at least one of your children?

There is a catch in ladder-climbing. Bigger-and-better for some of us becomes, if not impossible, at least unlikely. Between the golden promise of the 1950s and what has been for many the tarnished reality of the '80s, things changed. Today you may even compete with more people for fewer promotions and fewer higher places. You also struggle with the economy, finding it difficult to gain financial stability. In 1983, 44 percent of Americans had less than five thousand dollars in savings. Eleven percent had nothing in reserve. Upward mobility for them is not a reality.

Has this been your experience? Ladder-climbing didn't work out for you. So you changed careers, reoriented your life, and in general reduced the urge to be the best, the strongest, or the most powerful. At first this seemed to be the direct opposite of your basic ambitions. Trying to change what has been a way of life is never easy. Nor is it easier when it seems like failure.

Downward Mobility and Failure

Maybe you struggle with the phrase "downward mobility." The image that it generates is not entirely positive. That's true for me. I am a product of the "bigger and better" era. I need a new motto: "Not to win is not a sin!" Are you like that? Does the thought of failure catch hold of your insecurities? Ask yourself, "When is failure really failure?"

That's a good question. Some situations provide more dignity in not succeeding than in winning at all costs. Failure is not always failure. There are various kinds. One type I call a *noble* failure. Remember, General Robert E. Lee failed: General Ulysses Grant succeeded. But who are the great personalities of the Civil War? General Lee stands out as a leader of principle and integrity. Note this description of Lee's surrender at Appomattox Court House. As he rode past his troops for the final time "every hat was raised, and the bronzed faces of thousands of grim warriors were bathed in tears. . . . Devoted veterans pressed around the noble chief, trying to take his hand, touch his person, or even lay their hands upon his horse. . . . The general then with head bare, and tears flowing freely down his manly cheeks, bade adieu to the army" (*Civil War: The Years Asunder*, p. 182; Country Beautiful Corp., 1973). He gave his best for what he believed.

Jesus represents a *necessary* failure. His very purpose put him on a collision course with success as his world defined it. In failing he succeeded. In losing his life he saved it. There are some things an honorable person will not do. If the price for not doing them is failure, so be it. You may know what this means.

Todd was thirty-eight when he made the choice to resign his secure position and give up its future benefits. He could not support the growing deceptions of the firm. It meant his wife had to return to work while he spent eight months looking for a job. During that period their style of living was downgraded significantly. They sold luxury items that had become for them necessities. The results of this forced downward mobility were more positive than negative. Today, with a reduced salary and less of the good life, Todd reports, "We have never been as happy."

Downward mobility may be a different and a more profound kind of ambition. For you to choose to do or to become something other than what is expected may be the most successful achievement you can attain. You will have learned that bigger is not always best and that more is not necessarily the good life.

Downward Mobility and Success

A new definition of success is needed. To try to do something worthwhile and to fail is not a failure. You may be in this category. You set for yourself a goal that had integrity and possibility, but you didn't reach it. The fact that you tried is a success in itself. Real failure is failure to try, to risk. A pole-vaulter would never know how high he can jump if the bar wasn't raised until it was knocked down. So don't let yourself become immobile because you measure success only by the outcome.

Neither is the success valued by our culture the only kind. You can become preoccupied with only material things, the outward riches. Remember the intangible riches! The quality of your life is more important than the quantity of your possessions. That's the trap Jesus tried to keep us from. "For what shall it profit a man," he taught, "if he shall gain the whole world, and lose his own soul?" (Mark 8:36). The one who is rich in spiritual depth is the wealthy one.

You may be far more successful than you think. I have a friend who is a handyman in our community. His "fix-it" skills are in demand; he's successful. I know a widowed mother who raised five children by herself. She hasn't made *People* magazine, but she's successful. My parents never accumulated material wealth, but they faithfully shared their love for God in the skid rows and the Watts area of Los Angeles. They were successful! A pastor in my area has faithfully served a poverty community for ten years. By some standards, he has failed to get an appointment to an "affluent" church. To those who use his volunteer health clinics, he has awakened hope again in their lives. What marks the success of these persons? One criterion: their faithfulness. Faithfulness is the one quality that Jesus commended. He said, "Well done, thou good and faithful [*not successful*] servant."

Your life is designed to be invested in eternal endeavors. Being faithful in building hope and self-esteem in others does something for the kingdom of God and for you too. Jesus was clear; faithful servants are the successful ones.

Downward Mobility and Servanthood

The downward way is indeed expressed in servanthood. No one exemplified it more clearly than Jesus Christ. He moved from power to powerlessness, from strength to weakness, from security to vulnerability, from greatness to smallness, from receiving to serving. Both by word and by deed he set the pattern of the downward way. If we are to follow him, the choice is clear. Jesus said, "The disciple is not above his master, nor the servant above his lord" (Matt. 10:24). There it is again—servanthood.

Here's the tension. Your desire for personal growth and development is not wrong. Expressing your ambition to improve yourselves and your community is part of your creative capacity for change and growth. The problem is making ambition your end. Contrast the appetite that hungers for power and prestige with an attitude that seeks to be a servant. Think of the difference between people you know who crave for greatness and those who aspire to do all things well. But this presents us with some searching questions: "Am I willing to live at a lower standard of living if it means serving more effectively?" "Am I willing to labor at a position of less power and prestige if God calls me to something that results in that?" "Am I willing to strive faithfully to become a competent leader if God wants me there?" If you and I desire to be servants, the answer is yes.

I believe Jesus wants us to understand that servanthood is a daily vocation. You express your servanthood in the way you live your life and the way you treat people. When you give to the "least of these," Jesus said, you have done it unto me. In your business, your office, your classroom, your work station, your home—in every part of your world the concept and attitude of service to others is to be your undergirding motivation. An employee who works faithfully or a boss who respects people honors God. You and I serve God best when we serve one another.

The "Service" of Other-directed Ambition

Charles Swindoll, in his thoughtful book *Improving Your Serve: The Art of Unselfish Living,* observes, "Painful though it may be for us to admit it, we're losing touch with one another. The motivation to help, to encourage, yes to *serve* our fellowman is waning" (p. 17). You can do something about that. Right where you live there are persons who need to be touched by you.

Touch! Contact! Serving! Our society hungers for these. People caught up by high technology yearn for what John Naisbitt calls "high touch." He writes, "High tech/high touch is a formula I use to describe the way we have responded to technology. . . . Whenever new technology is introduced into society, there must be a counterbalancing human response—that is, *high touch*—or the technology is rejected" (*Megatrends,* p. 39; Warner Books, 1982). If Naisbitt is right, then our service is not only desired but vital. We need one another. We need to be in contact with one another, serving one another. Here are a few suggestions. Remember the old adage, "Practice makes perfect."

The Service of Creating

The most creative act that can happen to you is the renewal of your life. The Christian meaning of salvation is "re-creation." Belief in Jesus Christ and the recognition of your need for his forgiving grace transforms you into a "new creature," a new person. Your personality is renewed by your sincere repentance and acceptance of God's gift—Jesus Christ. For some the change is immediately apparent. For others the process is more extended. But for all there is the renewal of their creative capacity.

You can be creative! Actually, you are creative. The capacity to form something new and unique is inherent in all of us. And what you fashion can be your gift in response to God's love and renewing grace in your life. So don't get hung up on defining creativity as only acts or accomplishments of unusual importance. The works of the artist, the designer, the writer often get the public's attention, but they are only one type of creative expression.

I have a neighbor who works with crafts at youth camps and summer Bible schools. He prepares the wood pieces weeks in advance. He's creative. When you have taken time to prepare and present a nice dinner for your family and friends, you are being creative. Remember, Jesus said that a cup of cold water given to one of the least of these was given to him. Give yourself to the service of bringing forth newness. Identify what you are now doing and affirm it. Every day you can participate in new growth.

The Service of Listening

Shakespeare wrote, "It is the disease of not listening, the malady of not marking, that I am troubled withal" (*Henry IV*, Part 2). Observe conversations around you. Many times you will notice people talking to each other but not hearing each other. These conversations are like "dialogues of the deaf." The writer of Proverbs puts a high premium on hearing: "He that answereth a matter before he heareth it, it is folly and shame unto him" (Prov. 18:13). James 1:19 admonishes us to be swift to hear and slow to speak. Maybe God knew we needed two ears but only one mouth. Many situations can be resolved if people would spend twice the effort to listen than to respond. Married couples and families are helped by this ratio. I will never forget the words of my daughter when she was four years old. We were at the table eating and talking when she folded her arms and said, "I'm not talking. Nobody is listening." She taught me a lesson that day. It's no fun not to be heard.

Listening! Listening communicates that the person is valued and respected. Listening gives another your most cherished possession—time. But there is nothing passive about this service. Here are a few suggestions to improve your listening skills.

1. *Listen for feelings.* Have you asked a loved one recently, "How are you feeling?" Feelings are natural responses. You may have your facts wrong or be misperceiving the situation, but what you feel is real to you. So allow others to express their feelings. A husband once said to me in the presence of his wife, "She has no reason to feel insecure. I give her anything she needs." After working on some listening exercises, he came to learn about the pain of her past and became more understanding of her feelings. She became less insecure.

2. *Listen before responding.* When you are listening to someone, do you find yourself forming your responses before understanding what the person is saying? The fact that we all think five times faster than we talk makes this a greater temptation. Or perhaps your own concern about what you are going to say leaves you feeling anxious and self-conscious. You may then finish in your mind what you think the other person is going to say. Listening before responding is a way to say you really respect the person.

3. *Listen to behaviors.* Yes, behaviors talk. Over 70 per-

cent of the meaning of conversations is conveyed by the non-verbal cues and actions of the person talking. Good listeners learn to listen to the silent communications. Try observing what is being said through the voice tone, manner, and behavior of the person speaking. You will hear things you never heard before. Studies indicate that happier couples show more eye contact, laugh more, and touch each other more frequently, all wordless communications. When you listen to another person you are fulfilling Christ's call to "bear one another's burdens."

The Service of Acceptance

A Greek legend tells about Procrustes, who was a wicked robber. He had a nice bed for his guests, but they were forced to fit in it. Guests who were too tall would have their legs cut off. Those who were too short would be stretched. The one thing Procrustes wouldn't do was accept his guests as they were.

What a gift it is to accept some unpleasant aspect of those we love for long enough to let them decide it's time to change. Unfortunately, many people try to force those they love into preconceived molds. You want to be a servant to your spouse. Accept him or her for better or for worse. No more redeeming gift can you give than to give your loved ones acceptance. Accepting another is a service that can never be underestimated. In his book *Priceless Gifts,* Daniel Sugarman calls acceptance such a priceless gift. Here are some of his thoughts.

1. When we accept that life is always changing, we can live with change more creatively.
2. Difficulty in accepting our failures means difficulty in finding success.
3. When we accept the fact that the road isn't always going to be smooth, we are well on our way to smoothing out the road.

4. You can help people change by accepting them just the way they are.
5. Others will tend to accept you to the degree that you have accepted them.
6. When you accept someone's expression of anger, that person's anger is usually reduced.

The Service of Giving

Have you discovered the joy of giving? That joy is only a few steps away. The distance to a neighbor's house, the steps it takes to cross a room, the few moments needed to write a letter are all that separate you from knowing the joy of giving. Who in your life would appreciate a call from you? Which neighbor needs a boost by a visit or a word of encouragement? Have you been wanting to invite someone special over for dinner? When you do something for another, you enjoy the experience that "it is more blessed to give than to receive" (Acts 20:35).

Alfred Adler confirms the importance of giving. Adler writes, "The only individuals who can really meet and master the problems of life . . . are those who show in their striving a tendency to enrich all others, who go ahead in such a way that others benefit also" (*What Life Should Mean to You*, p. 69; Grosset & Dunlap, 1931). It's true. Your life takes on new meaning when you invest yourself in others.

My daughter had knee surgery the month before her senior year in high school. This was a low time for us all. She was out of school for eight weeks and was not a cheerleader for six months. I saw the healing power of giving during this time. A woman in our neighborhood arrived at our door with a bag of individually wrapped gifts, instructing my daughter, "You are to open one each day!" She gave her the best one-a-day medicine possible.

Look for ways to support, to encourage, to build up, and to give to another. Enjoying a good laugh with a shut-in wastes little energy. Walking in the park with a loved one doesn't cost much. Sharing a sunset with a lonely person isn't tiring. And the more smiles you give away, the more they are sent back to you. Practice your service of giving.

The Service of Compassion

Compassion is a quiet power. The word comes from the Latin for "suffer with." It is the most healing of all human emotions. Read again the story of the good Samaritan. Compassion was the difference. Notice who had it. The Samaritan didn't just observe the wounded man, he identified with him. Furthermore, he had courage. That's needed when you decide to care for another. Courage translates your concerns into actions. You can't let the fear of getting involved hinder you if you are going to be caring.

But there was something else this Samaritan had. He was in the habit of helping. Going to the aid of the man on the Jericho road was not an isolated incident. He did what he did because that's what he had been doing. Through the years he had responded to the needs around him. How? In the same way you and I can, by endless repetition of small deeds. By giving someone your help—if you can. By going the extra mile—occasionally. By accepting a fair share of community responsibility—when you can manage it. Any one of these acts may not seem like much, but added together you become a Samaritan yourself.

Ambition! What a marvelous gift! You and I are created with a capacity to develop it. We nurture it in the early years of our youth. And we mature it in the crucible of our life's experiences.

Ambition! Consecrate it unto God and we will honor it.

Ambition! Couch it in deeds of service to others and we will enjoy its creativity.

Ambition! Celebrate it in the context of thankfulness and worship and we will enhance its beauty.

This, then, is my desire for you and me, that our highest ambition will always be to "press toward the mark for the prize of the high calling of God in Christ Jesus" (Phil. 3:14).

And this is my prayer for us:

> Now the God of peace, that brought again from the dead our Lord Jesus, that great shepherd of the sheep, through the blood of the everlasting covenant, make [us] perfect in every good work to do his will, working in [us] that which is well-pleasing in his sight, through Jesus Christ; to whom be glory for ever and ever. Amen. (Heb. 13:20-21)

Questions for Thought and Discussion

Chapter 1
Let's Take a Look at Our Ambitions

1. Complete "Ambition is . . ." ten times. Compare your list with that of two other persons. Write a combined definition.

2. Is ambition learned or inherited? How is it encouraged or hindered in children? What determines whether it is good or bad?

3. What awakens your ambition? Identify one influence each from your past, present, and future that shapes your ambition.

Chapter 2
Ambition Undisciplined

1. List synonyms for ambition. Do the words reflect negative or positive meanings? Why? Compare your list and feelings.

2. How did your background enhance or hinder your ambition? Give examples. How are children hurried today? Describe ways parents push children. Discuss ways parents can reduce this pressure.

Chapter 3
Ambition Self-directed

1. Describe the rich man's ambition in Luke 12:13-21. Review the principles he violated. How could you change the story to make ambition a friend?

2. Cite biblical and contemporary examples of ambition that consumes or exploits others.

3. Describe a strategy that will mature your spirituality and one that will develop simplicity in your life.

Chapter 4
Ambition Misdirected

1. Read Matthew 20:20-28. Imagine you are the mother. What are you feeling? What motivates your request?

2. What are signs of being driven? When do you feel driven? Why?

3. How does personality affect ambition? When do you feel inferior? What might be the reasons for that feeling? What relaxes you?

Chapter 5
Ambition Inner-directed

1. What is Jesus teaching in Matthew 15:1-20? How do the principles in this passage apply to your situation?

2. What does it mean to "be"? Discuss ways to develop "being."

3. What has helped you to develop your inner life? Choose one discipline you would like to follow. Tell how you will do it.

Chapter 6
Ambition Other-directed

1. Define a servant, downward mobility, and success. List ways you are creative.

2. Identify your neighbors by name. Describe ways you can serve each. Pick one and do something specific for him or her today.

Selected Bibliography

Blaine, Graham. *Youth and the Hazards of Affluence.* Harper & Row, 1966.

Bonhoeffer, Dietrich. *Life Together.* Harper & Row, 1954.

Dobson, James. *Hide or Seek.* Fleming H. Revell Co., 1971.

Elkind, David. *The Hurried Child: Growing Up Too Fast Too Soon.* Addison-Wesley Publishing Co., 1981.

Epstein, Joseph. *Ambition: The Secret Passion.* Penguin Books, 1980.

Erikson, Erik. *Childhood and Society.* W. W. Norton & Co., 1950.

Foster, Richard J. *Freedom of Simplicity.* Harper & Row, 1981.

Friedman, Meyer, and Rosenman, Ray H. *Type A Behavior and Your Heart.* Alfred A. Knopf, 1974.

Gordon, Arthur. *A Touch of Wonder.* Jove/Harcourt Brace Jovanovich, 1974.

Greenleaf, Robert K. *Servant Leadership.* Paulist Press, 1977.

Lasch, Christopher. *The Culture of Narcissism.* W. W. Norton & Co., 1978.

Linkletter, Art. *Yes, You Can!* Simon & Schuster, 1979.

May, Rollo. *The Courage to Create.* W. W. Norton & Co., 1975.

Missildine, Hugh. *Your Inner Child of the Past.* Simon & Schuster, 1963.

Oates, Wayne. *Workaholics, Make Laziness Work for You.* Abingdon Press, 1978.

Postman, Niel. *The Disappearance of Childhood.* Delacorte Press, 1982.

Sanford, John A. *The Kingdom Within.* J. B. Lippincott Co., 1970.

Seamands, David. *Problem Solving in the Christian Family.* Carol Stream, Ill.: Creation House, 1975.

————. *Putting Away Childish Things.* Victor Books, 1982.

Sugarman, Daniel A. *Priceless Gifts.* Macmillan Publishing Co., 1978.

Swindoll, Charles R. *Improving Your Serve: The Art of Unselfish Living.* Word Books, 1981.

Wagner, Maurice E. *The Sensation of Being Somebody.* Zondervan Publishing House, 1975.